THE SECRET TO A GOOD LIFE
BOB & ROBERTA SMITH
ROYAL ACADEMY OF ARTS

DEIRDRE BORLASE

met my father Frederick Brill at the Royal Collage of Art in 1943 where he made this painting

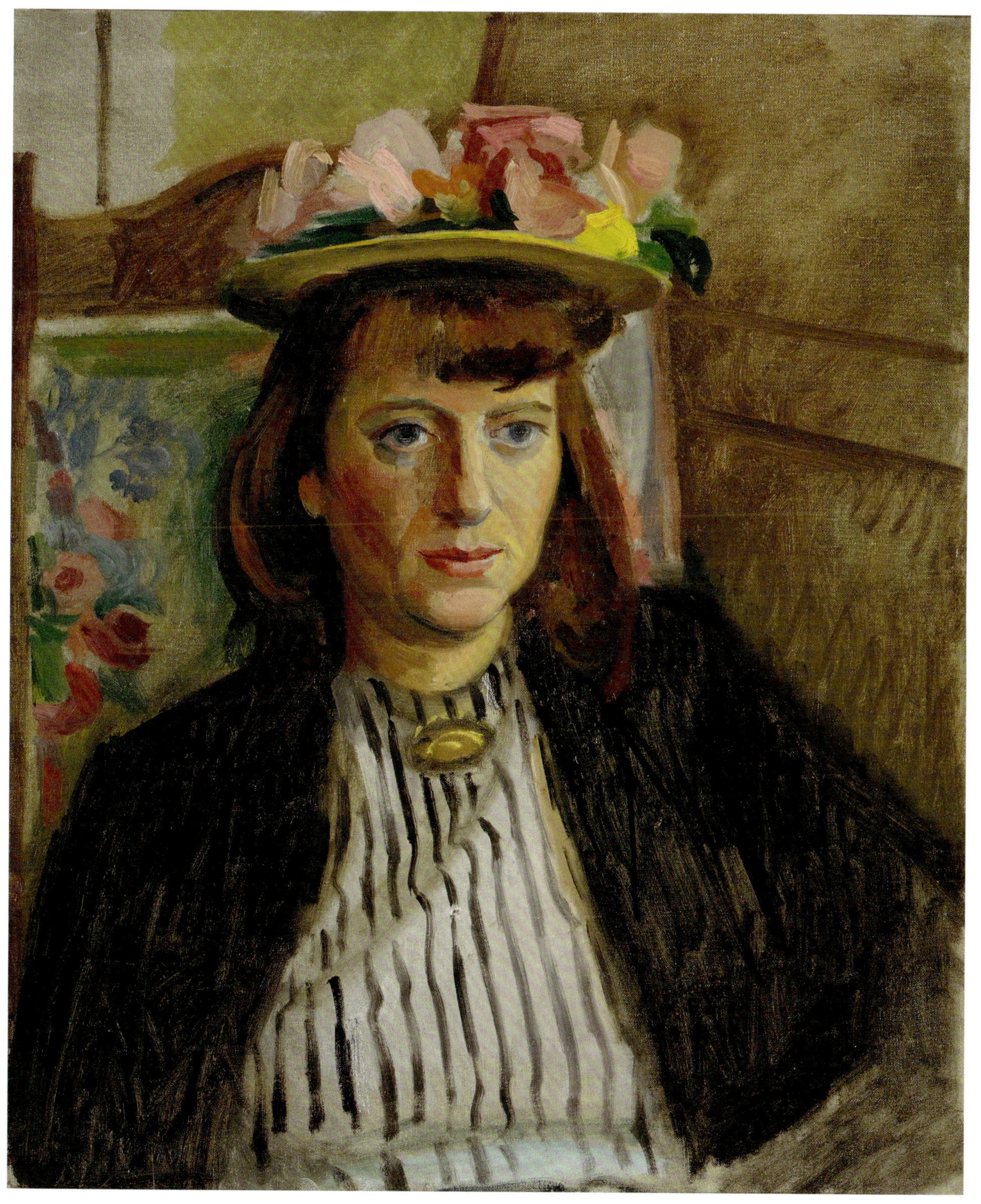

MY MOTHER DEIRDRE BORLASE TAUGHT ME TO DRAW

BOTH MY
PARENTS
WERE
ARTISTS

MY FATHER'S
ABILITY TO
DRAW
TRANSFORMED
OUR LIVES

BY THE TIME
I WAS BORN HE
WAS RUNNING
CHELSEA SCHOOL
OF ART

MY FATHER STARTED HIS WORKING LIFE IN A BLUE BAND MARGERINE FACTORY

HIS FATHER
SOLD VEGETABLES
ON NORTH END Rd
MARKET IN
FULHAM

MY MOTHER
DREW
EVERY
DAY OF HER
LIFE

SHE GREW
UP IN MARGATE
BETWEEN
THE
WARS

DEIRDRE
DREW IN
SCHOOL
ONCE WHEN SHE
WAS DRAWING

WHEN SHE SHOULD HAVE

BEEN STUDYING MATHS
HER TEACHER TOOK
HER SKETCHBOOK AND
THREW IT IN THE OPEN
FIRE WHICH WAS
HEATING THE
CLASS ROOM

FROM THEN
ON SHE SAW
DRAWING AS
HER
RIGHT

SHE THOUCHT ART WAS
SOMETHING PEOPLE IN
AUTHORITY WERE
FRIGHTENED BY
AND NOT
UNDERSTAND

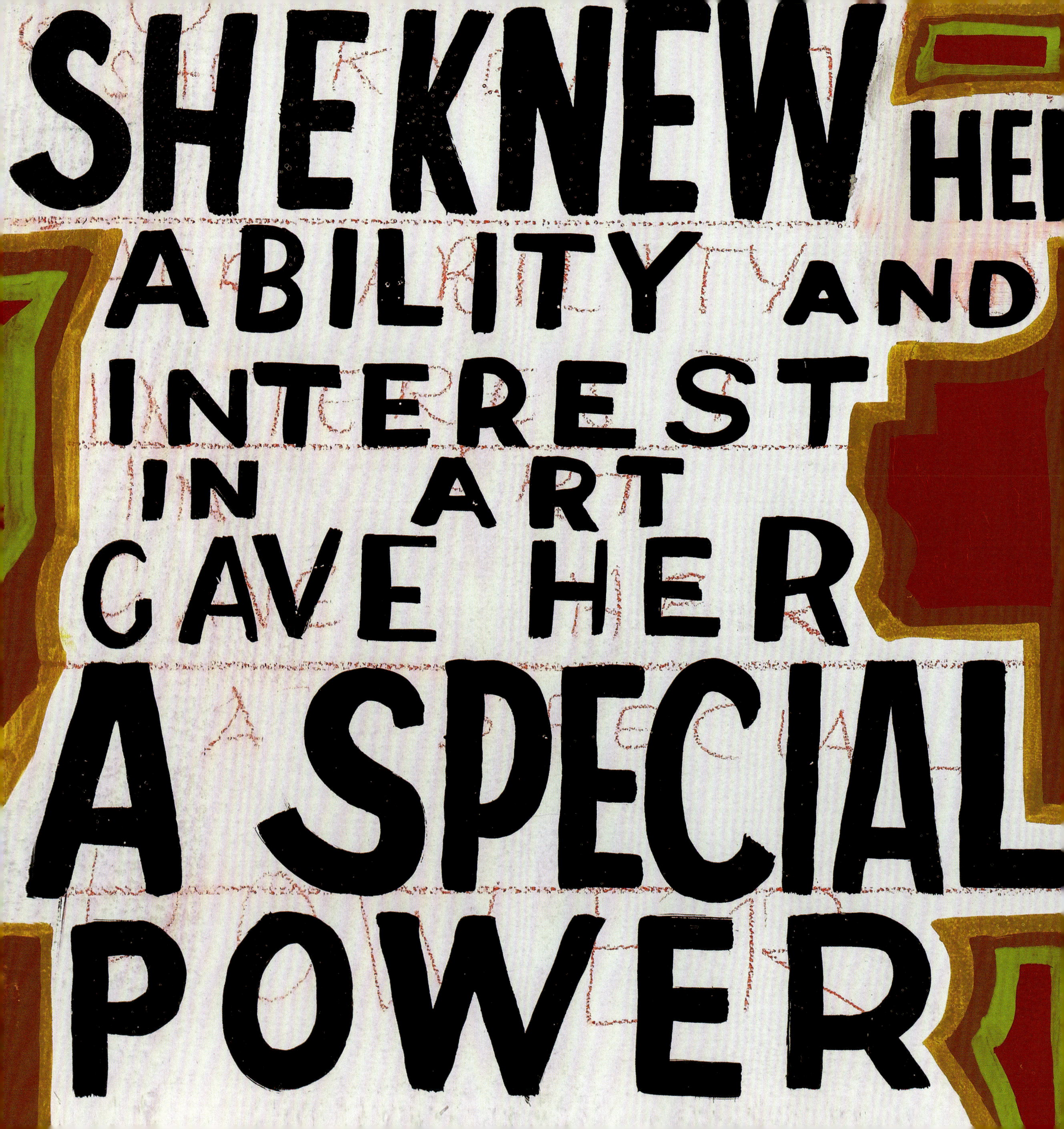

SHE KNEW HER ABILITY AND INTEREST IN ART GAVE HER A SPECIAL POWER

SHE WENT TO MARGATE ART SCHOOL. AS A VISUALLY MINDED YOUNG WOMAN IN THE 1930S SHE WAS STEERED TOWARDS DRESSMAKING RATHER THAN MAKING PAINTINGS

IN 1940 THE EVACUATION
OF DUNKIRK LEAD
TO SOLDIERS BEING
BILLETED WHERE
MY MOTHER LIVED
MANY CIVILIANS LEFT
MARGATE IN FEAR
OF IMMINENT
INVASION

MY MOTHER REMEMBERS BOARDING A TRAIN TO LONDON WITH SOLDIERS. ON THE TRIP O LONDON SHE REMEMBERS BACK GARDENS WERE SHROUDED IN BANNERS WELCOMING SOLDIERS BACK TO BRITAIN

DEIRDRE ENROLLED AT BROMLEY ART SCHOOL IN 1943. SHE WON A SCHOLARSHIP TO THE ROYAL COLLEGE TO STUDY GRAPHIC ART

THE ROYAL COLLEGE HAD BEEN EVACUATED TO AMBLESIDE IN CUMBRIA

ONCE AT THE ROYAL COLLEGE DEIRDRE DECIDED SHE WANTED TO TRANSFER FROM GRAPHIC ART TO MAKING PAINTINGS

CONSIDERABLE RESISTANCE TO THIS MOVE WAS MADE CLEAR BY THE COLLEGE, PAINTING WAS SERIOUS STUFF AND NOT FOR PEOPLE LIKE MY MOTHER.

BUT EVENTUALLY SHE WAS ALLOWED TO TRANSFER. GILBERT SPENCER TAUGHT HER. SPENCER'S MURAL DECORATES THE DOWNSTAIRS CAFE AT THE ROYAL ACADEMY

AT THE ROYAL COLLEGE OF ART SHE MET MY FATHER. AT THE END OF THE WAR THE R.C.A RETURNED TO EXHIBITION ROAD. MY MOTHER GRADUATED THERE IN 1946

AFTER THE WAR
MY PARENTS WOULD
SUBMIT THEIR 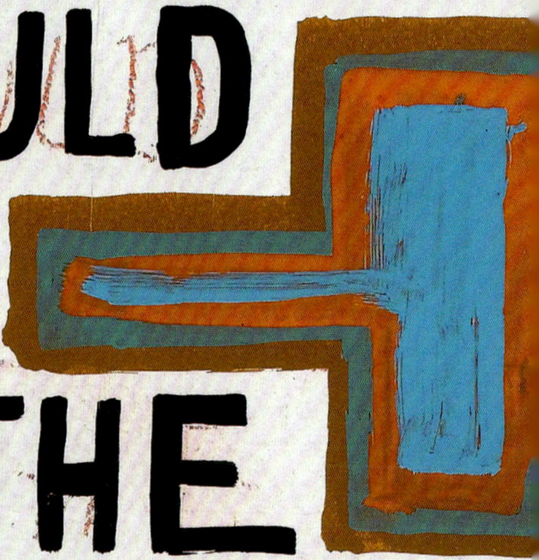
PAINTINGS TO THE
ROYAL ACADEMY SUMMER
EXHIBITION. EACH YEAR
THERE WOULD BE
JUBILATION OR
PROFOUND DISAPPOINTME

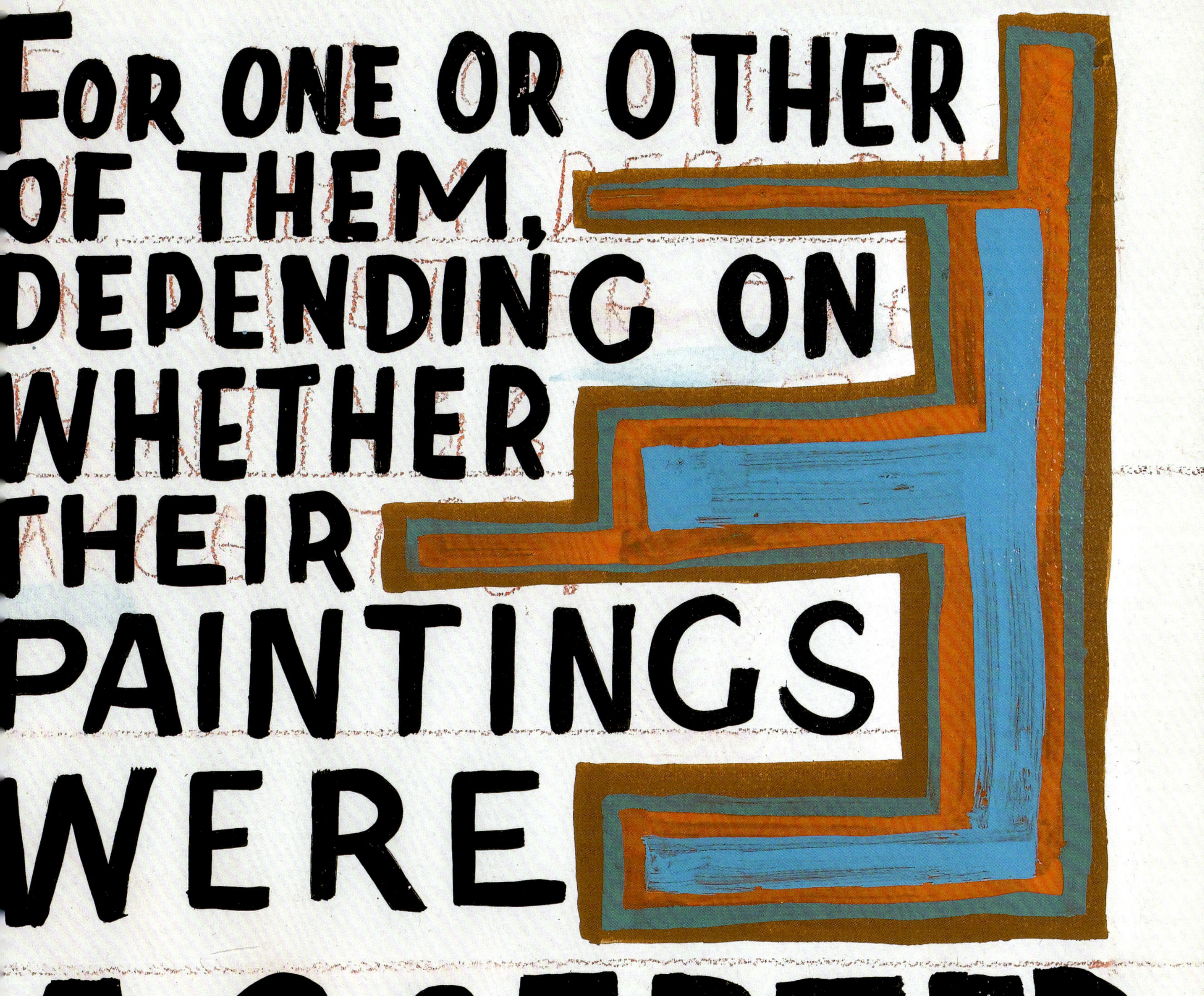

FOR ONE OR OTHER
OF THEM,
DEPENDING ON
WHETHER
THEIR
PAINTINGS
WERE
ACCEPTED

MY MOTHER REALISED THA
SHE WAS MORE CERTAIN OF GETTIN
HER WORK INTO THE SHOW
IF SHE SIGNED HER PAINTING
SIMPLY 'D. BORLASE' RATHER
THAN WRITING HER FULL
NAME DEIRDRE
BORLASE

THERE WAS A
SENCE THAT
ALL ART WAS
A MALE
PRESERVE

SHE FELT DISCRIMINATED AGAINST AND BEGAN TO UNDERSTAND AND VOICE TO HER FRIENDs THAT THE ROYAL ACADEMY WAS A MISOGYNISTIC INSTITUTION

HOWEVER

ONCE IN THE SHOW SHE ENJOYED ALL THE PARTIES AND SHE WAS FAR MORE SUCCESSFUL THAN MY FATHER IN SELLING HER WORK

OVER THIRTY YEARS OF SELLING HER PAINTINGS SHE BUILT UP A CONSIDERABLE FOLLOWING WHICH WAS ANCHORED IN THE SUCCESS OF HER WORKS IN THE SUMMER EXHIBITION

MY FATHER
RESENTED MY
MOTHER'S
SUCCESS

I CAN ONLY
REMEMBER ONE TIME
WHEN THEY BOTH GOT
INTO THE SUMMER SHOW
AND AS A FAMILY
WE ALL HAPPILY
ATTENDED THE
PRIVATE VIEW

EVEN THAT YEAR
MY FATHER WAS
GRUMPY
BECAUSE HIS
PAINTING DID
NOT SELL

AT THE
HEIGHT OF
MY MOTHER'S
SUCCESS SHE
WAS SELLING

THOUSANDS OF
POUNDS WORTH
OF PAINTINGS
AND PRINTS
EACH YEAR

SELLING ART
BECAME HER MAIN
SOURCE OF
INCOME. SHE
NEVER BRAGGED

ABOUT HER
SUCCESS BUT MY
MOTHER HAD
BEATEN THE
SYSTEM TWICE

SHE HAD BROKEN
THROUGH THE CLASS
BARRIER AND SHE HAD
BECOME SUCCESSFUL
IN A MANS WORLD

MY PARENTS GENERATION WERE TAUGHT TO RENDER THE WORLD WITH ACCURACY AND TO

CAREFULLY INSPECT
COLOUR BOTH MY
PARENTS WERE ARTISTS
BUT THEY WERE NOT
BOHEMIANS.

For them art was deeply serious work, it had its roots in scholarship and skills that were born in the 19th century

IN THE 1960s ARTISTS LIKE MY PARENTS WERE LARGELY MADE UNFASHIONABLE AND

REDUNDANT BY PO PART AND MODERNISM. MY PARENTS HAD STUDIED IN AMBLESIDE IN THE NEXT VALLEY TO WHERE

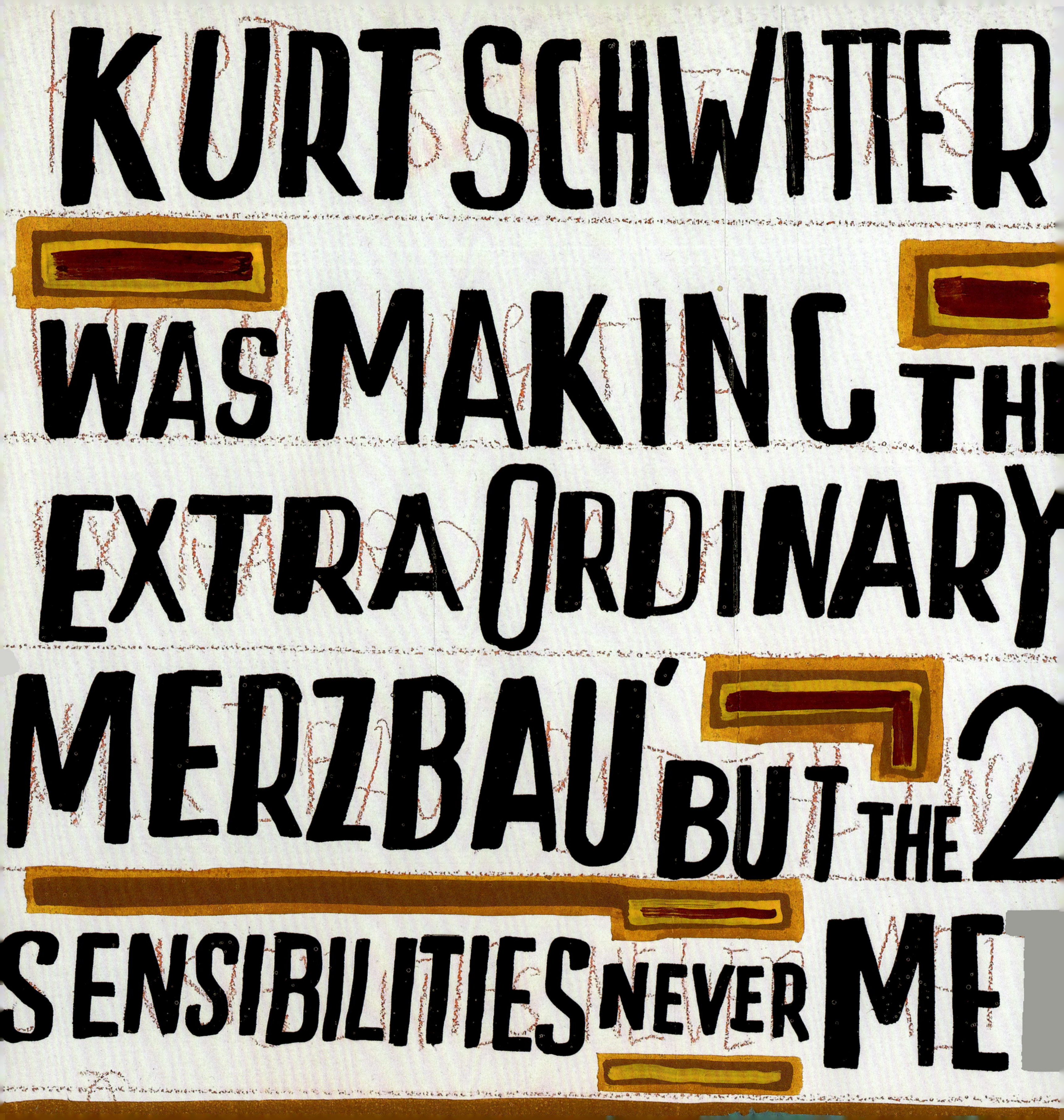

KURT SCHWITTER WAS MAKING THE EXTRAORDINARY MERZBAU' BUT THE 2 SENSIBILITIES NEVER MET ME

IF THEY HAD MET
PERHAPS MY PARENTs
WOULD HAVE BEEN BETTER
EQUIPPED TO DEAL
WITH THE CHANGES IN ART
IN POSTWAR BRITAIN

DURRING THOSE YEAR,
THE ROYAL ACADEMY
SUMMER EXHIBITION
WAS LIKE A CLUB
IN WHICH ARTISTS WHO
HAD HAD THEIR
WORLD TURNED
UPSIDE DOWN COULD
MEET UP AND
SHARE NOTES

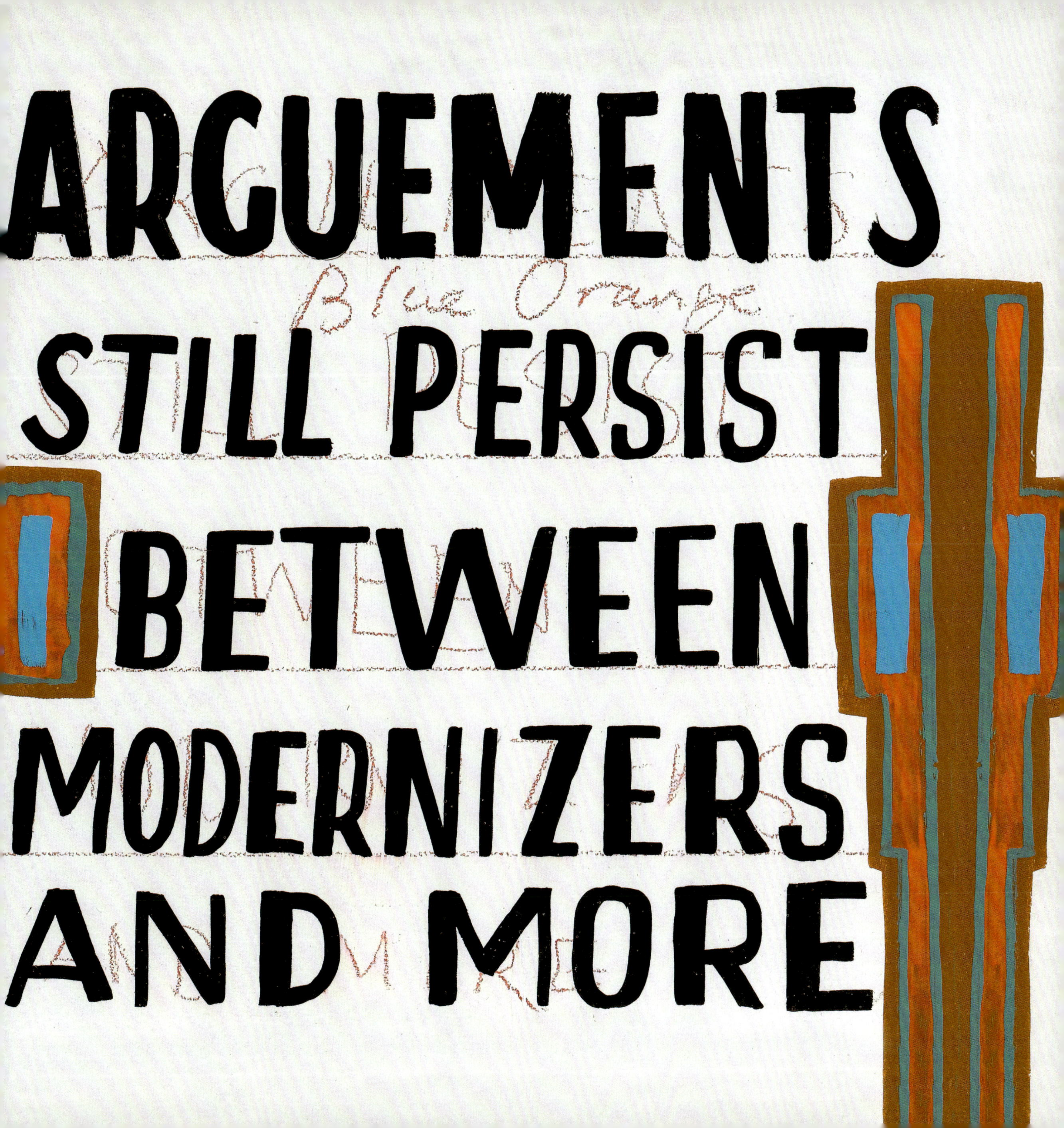

ARGUEMENTS STILL PERSIST BETWEEN MODERNIZERS AND MORE

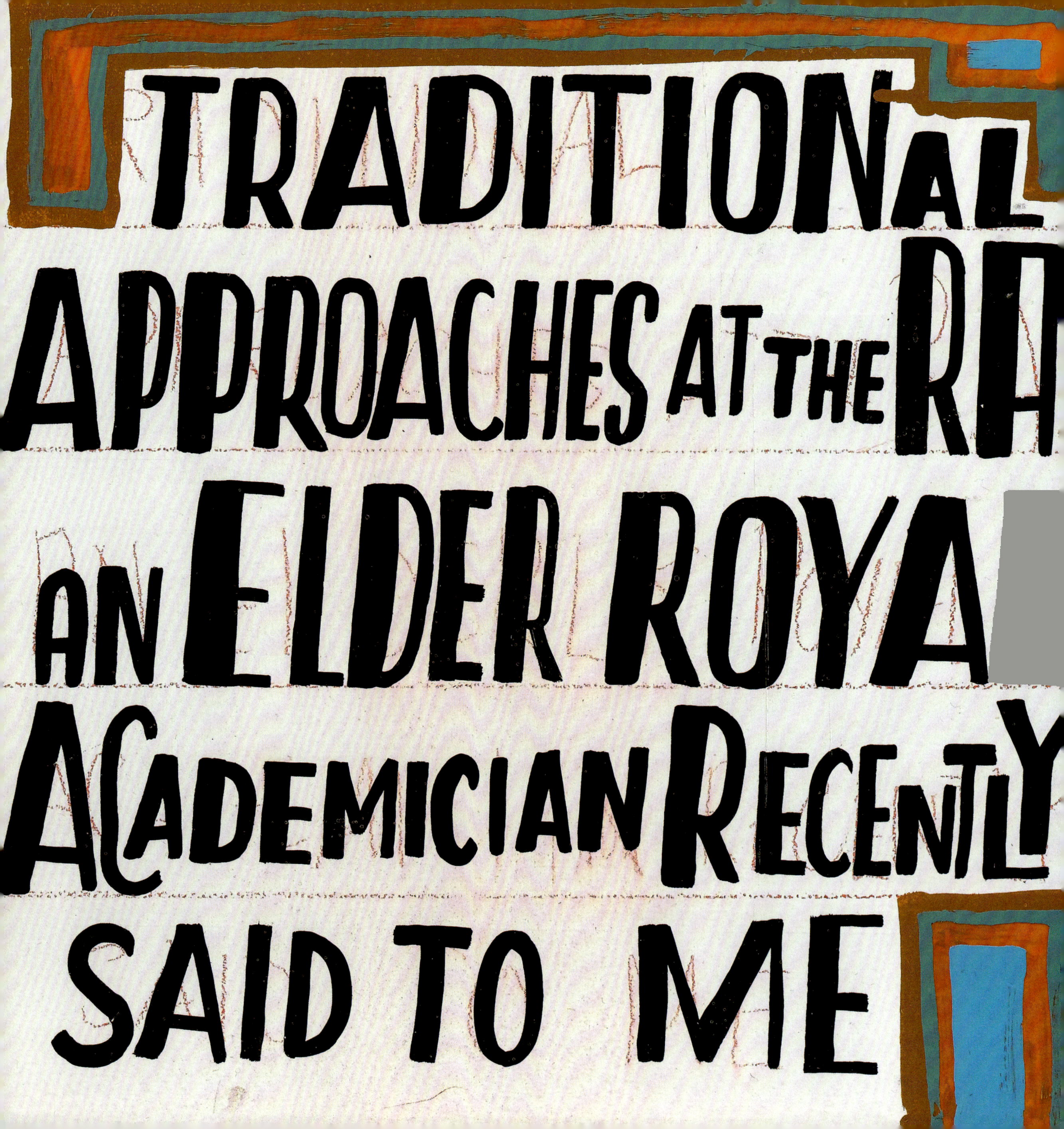

TRADITIONAL
APPROACHES AT THE RA

"AN ELDER ROYA
ACADEMICIAN RECENTLY
SAID TO ME

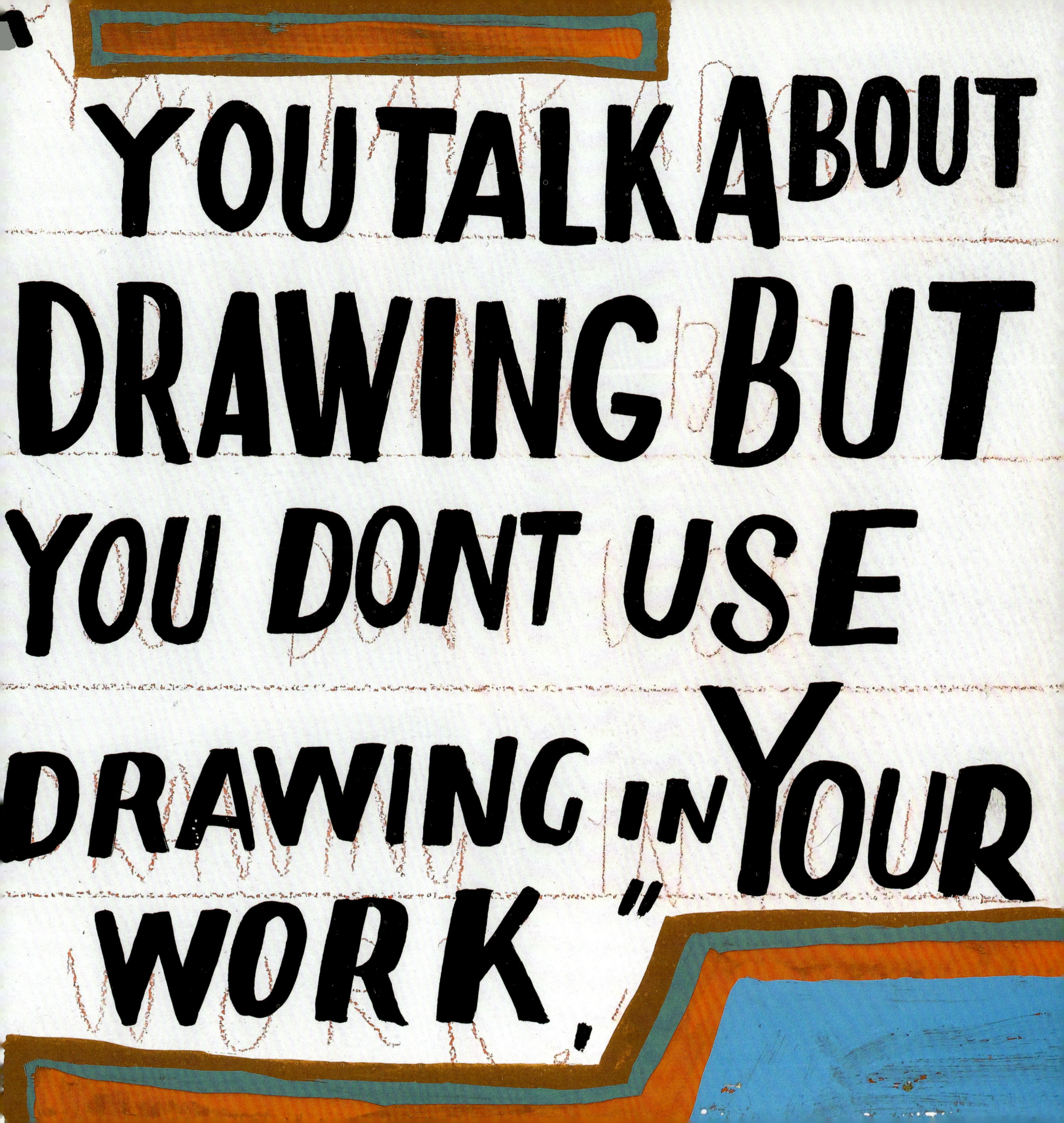

'YOU TALK ABOUT DRAWING BUT YOU DONT USE DRAWING IN YOUR WORK."

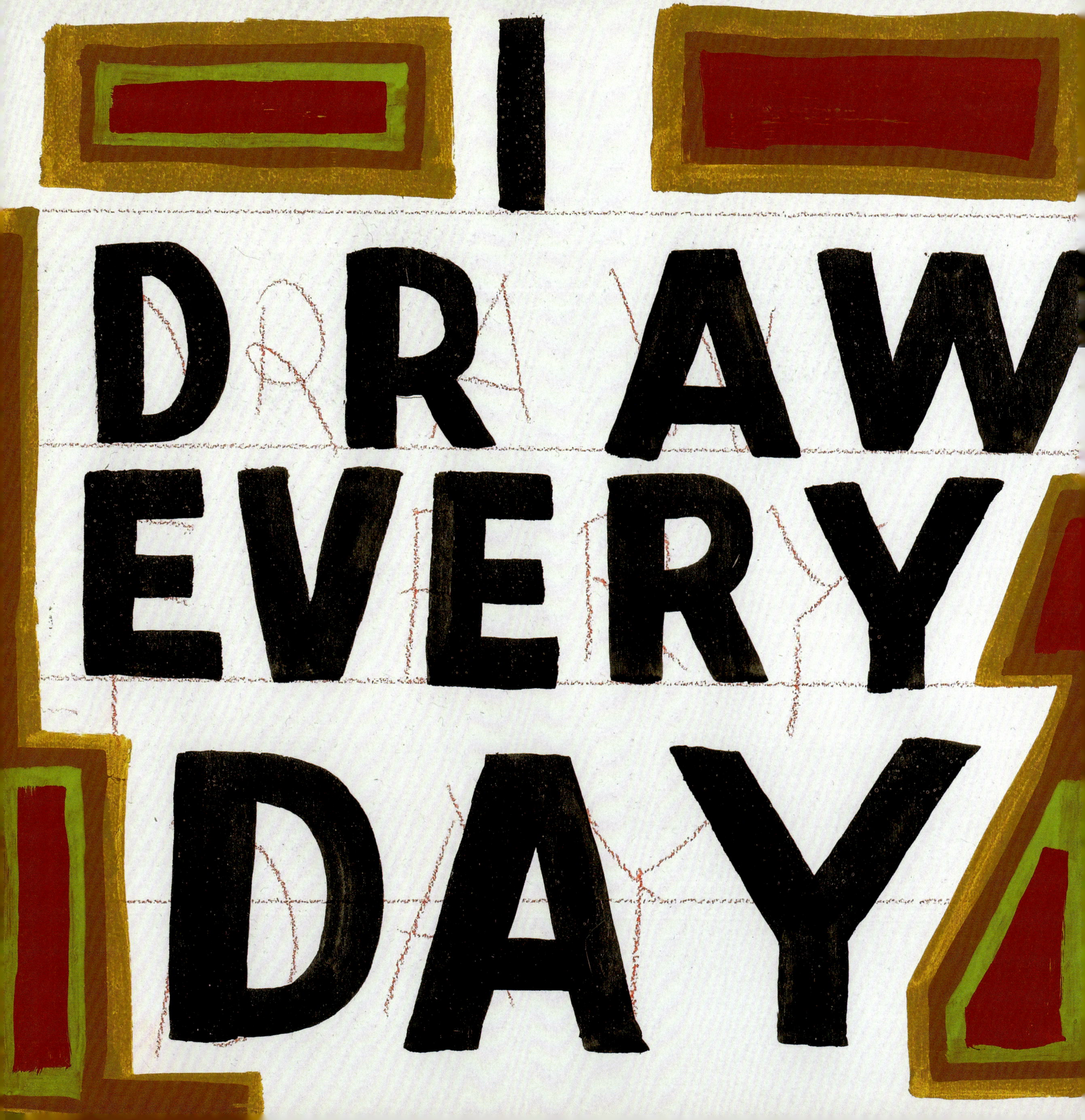

I DRAW EVERY DAY

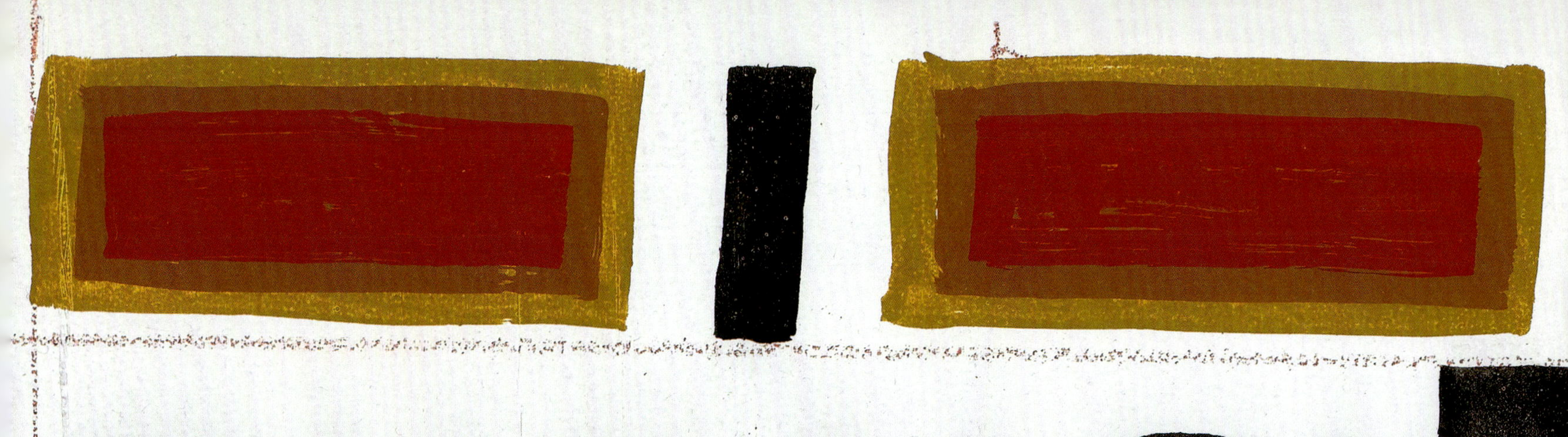

I THOUGHT ABOUT WHAT DRAWING IS

DRAWING IS ABOUT MAKING YOUR MARK

GIVE A CHILD
A BLANK
SHEET OF
PAPER AND
SOME PAINT

AND YOU ARE ASKING THAT CHILD TO CONSTRUCT THEIR WORLD

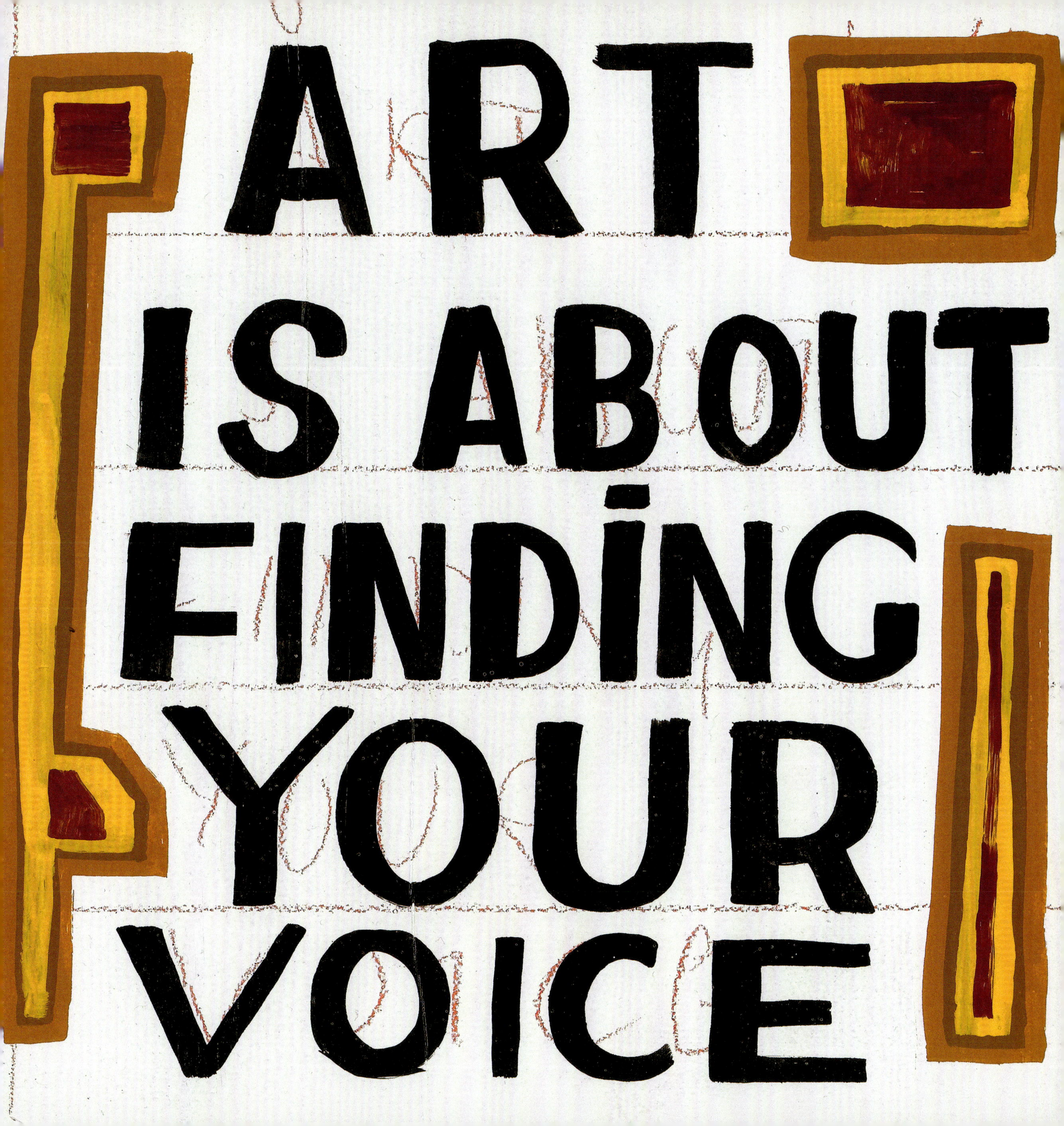

ART
IS ABOUT
FINDING
YOUR
VOICE

AND FEELIN' CONFIDENT TO USE YOUR VOICE

YOUR
VOICE
NEEDS
YOU

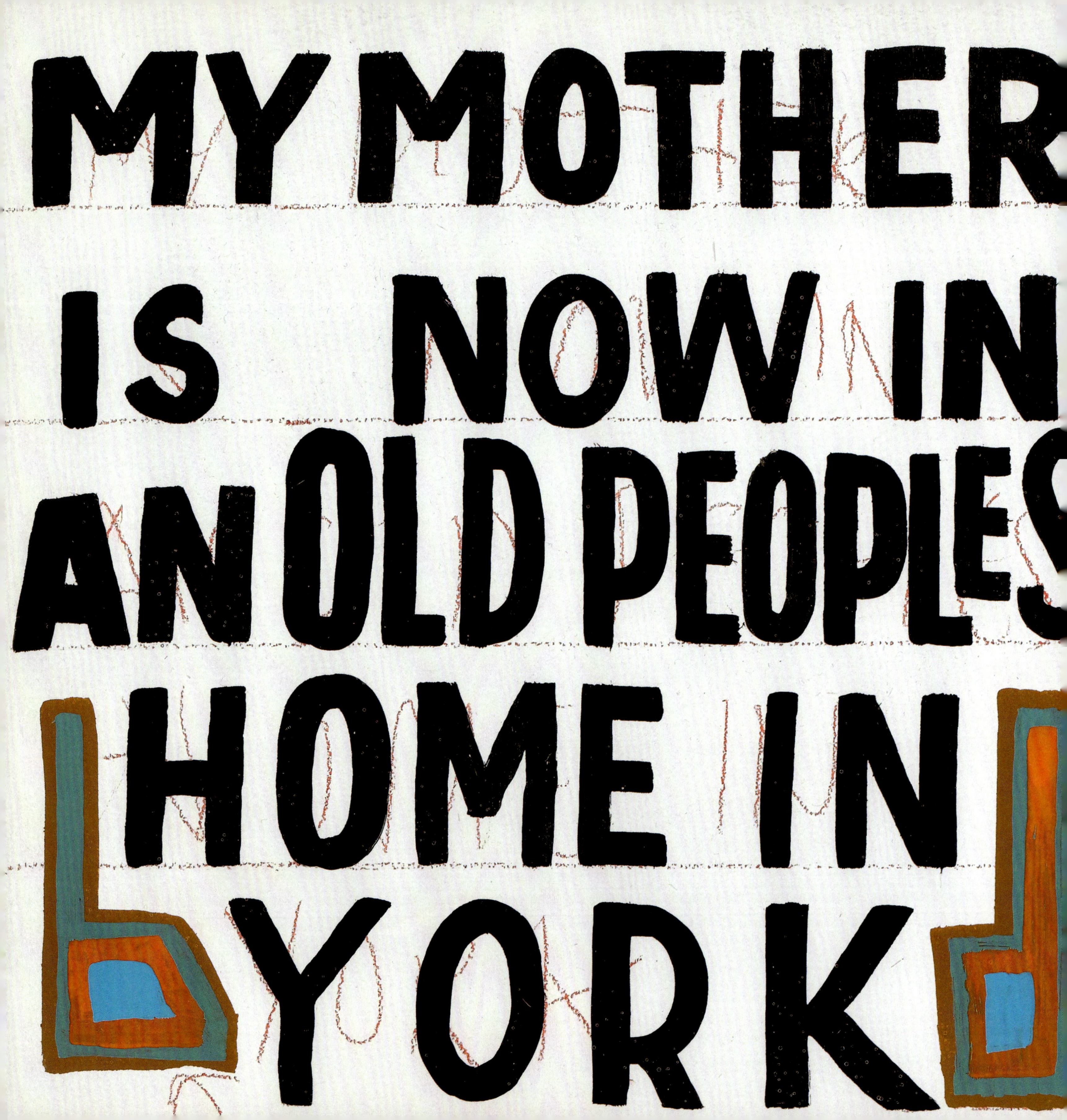

MY MOTHER
IS   NOW IN
AN OLD PEOPLES
HOME IN
YORK

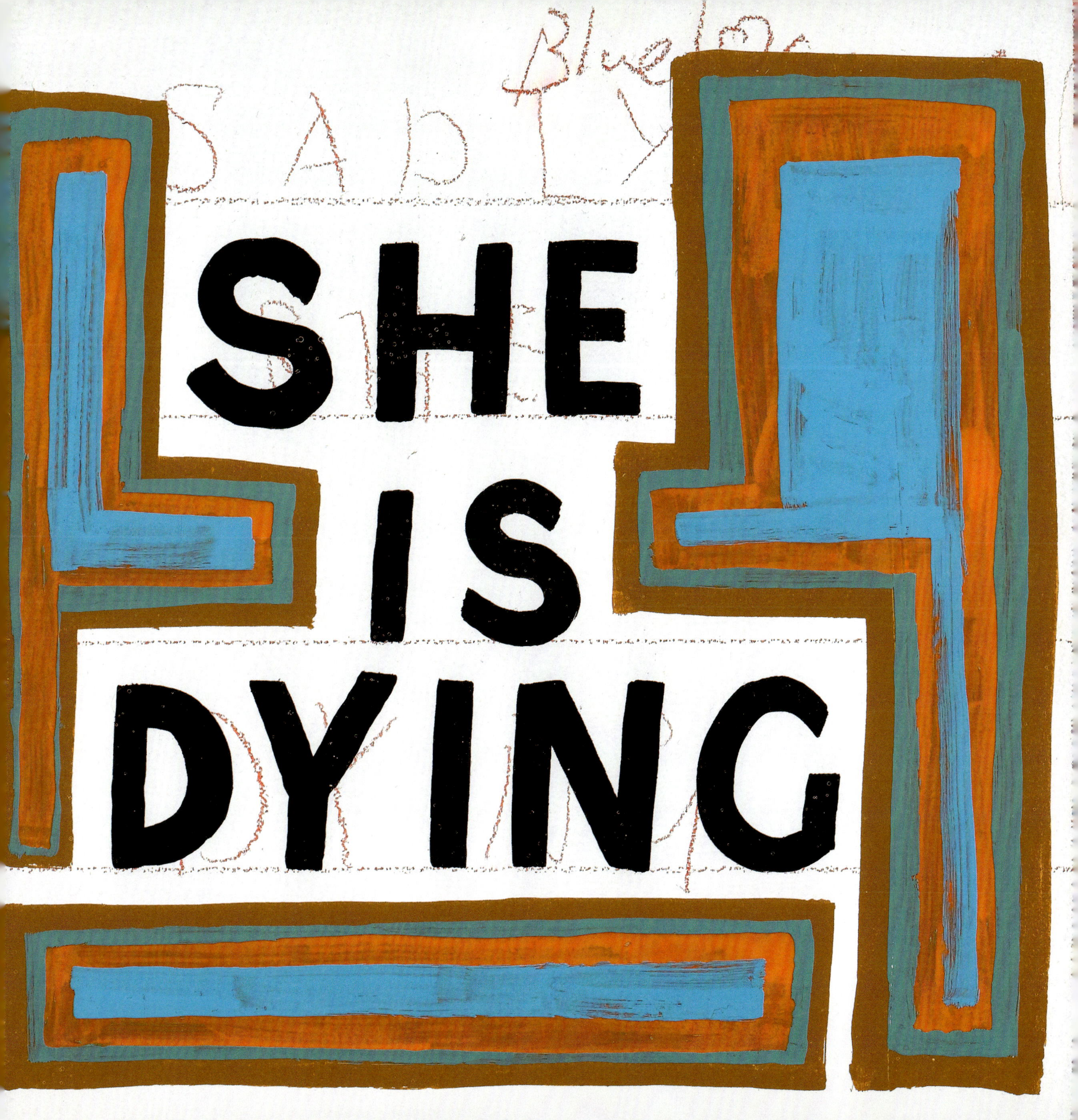
SHE
IS
DYING

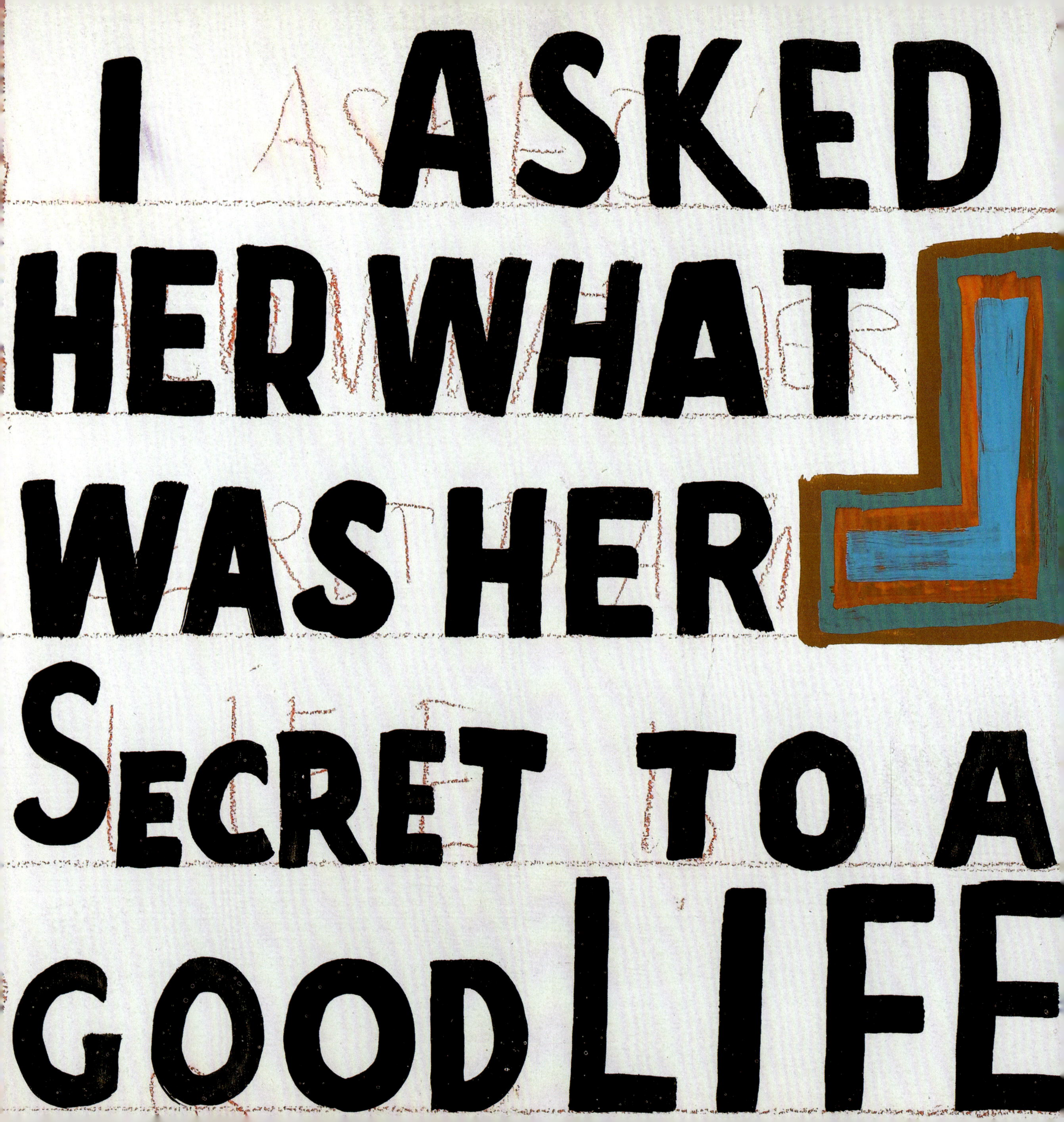

I ASKED
HER WHAT
WAS HER
SECRET TO A
GOOD LIFE

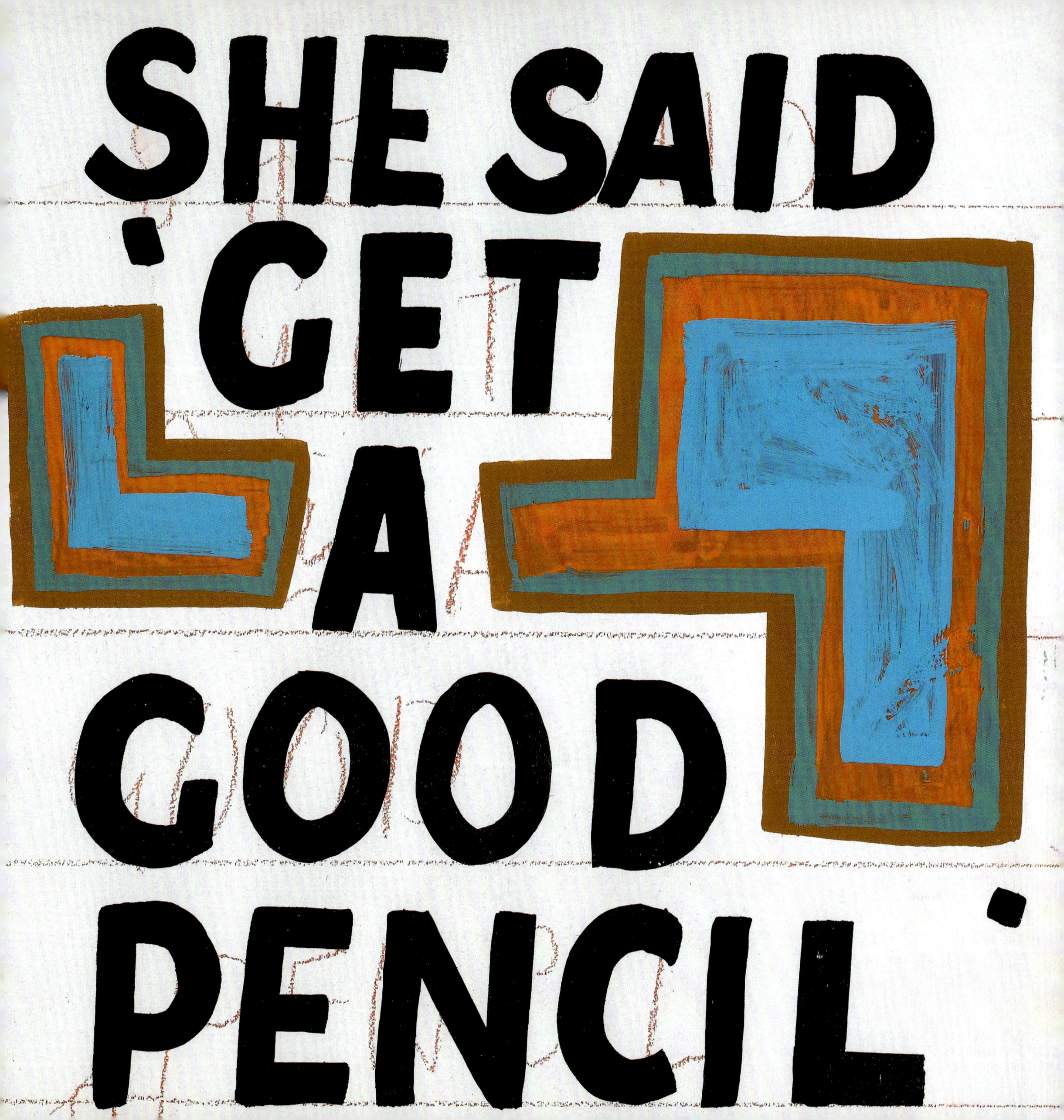

SHE SAID
'GET
A
GOOD
PENCIL'

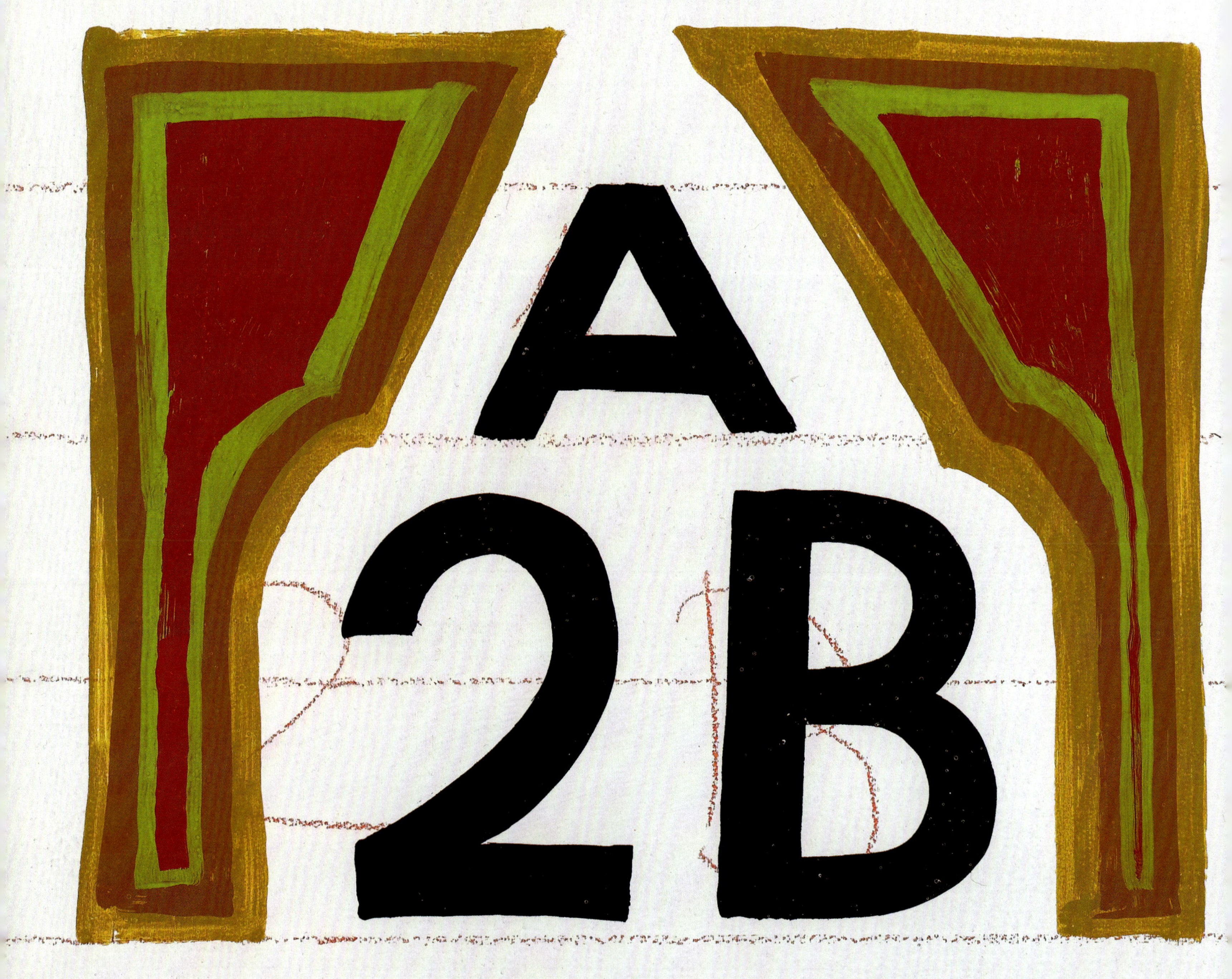
A
2B

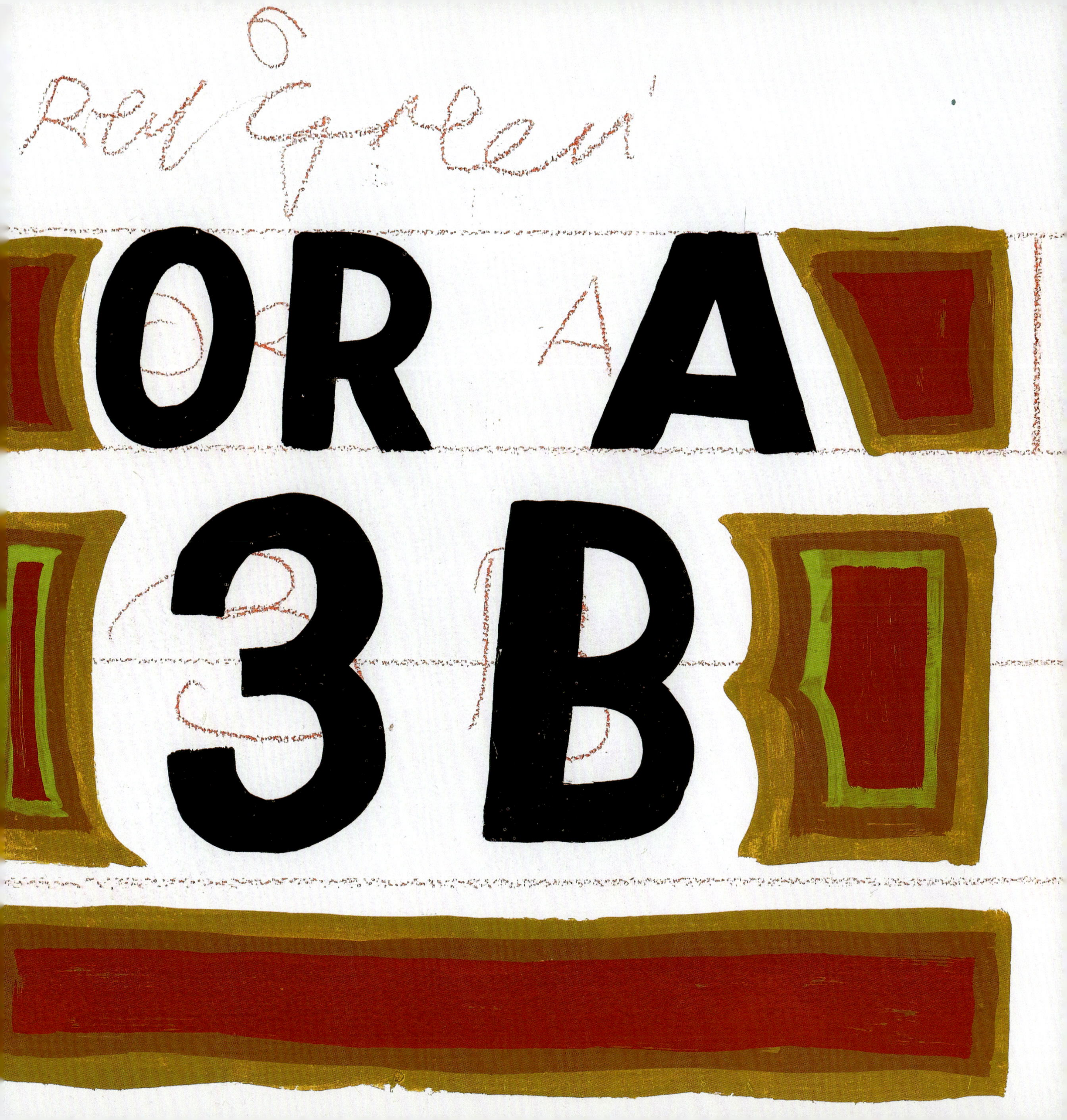

Red green
OR A
3 B

NOT an HB

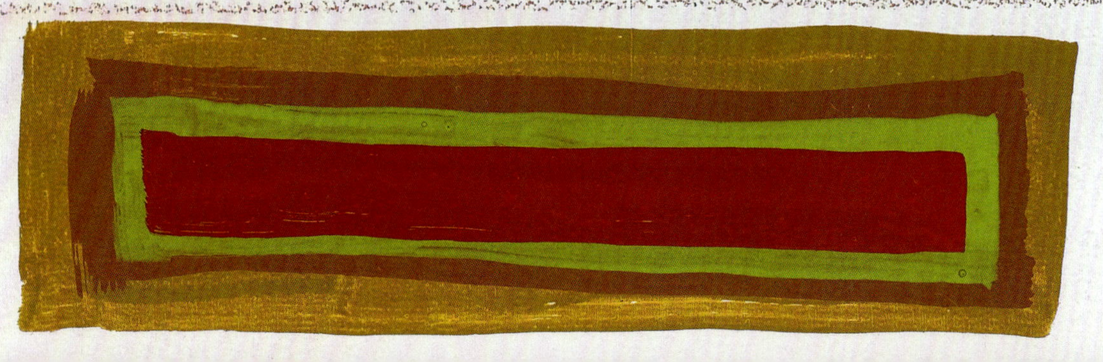

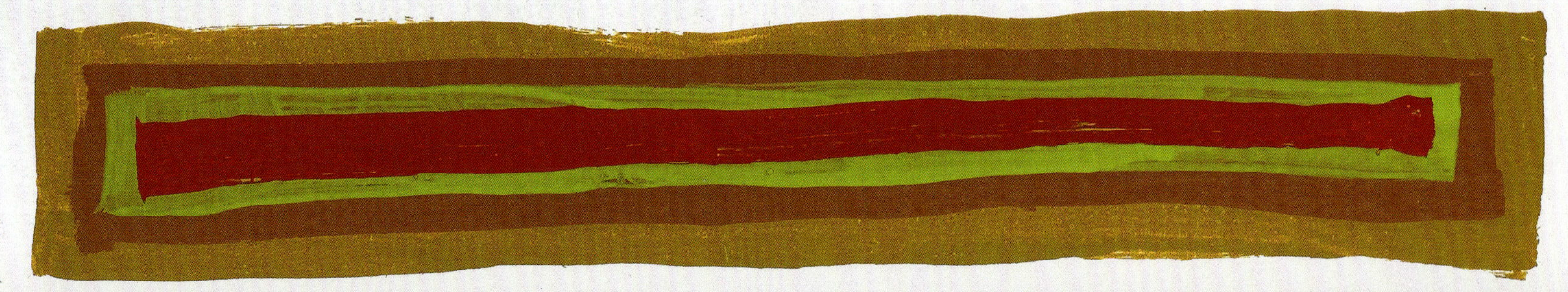

HB'S ARE
FOR
ARCHITECTS

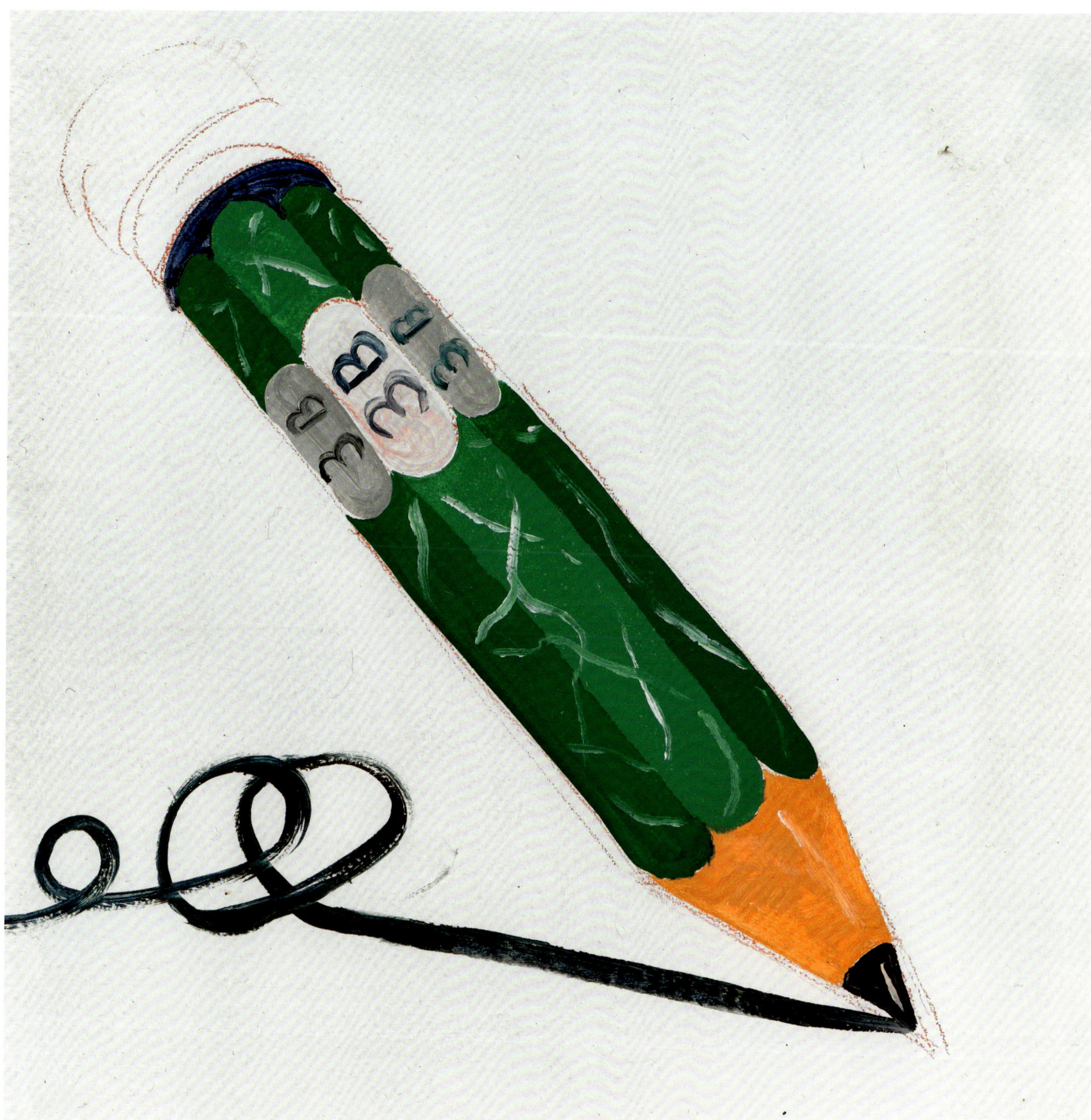

AMBLESIDE 1944

This was painted when Deirdre was a student at the Royal College of ART during its 'Wartime evacuatio It depicts 'DIG FOR VICTORY' allotment as seen from the "SALUTATION" Hotel, the then location of the RCA

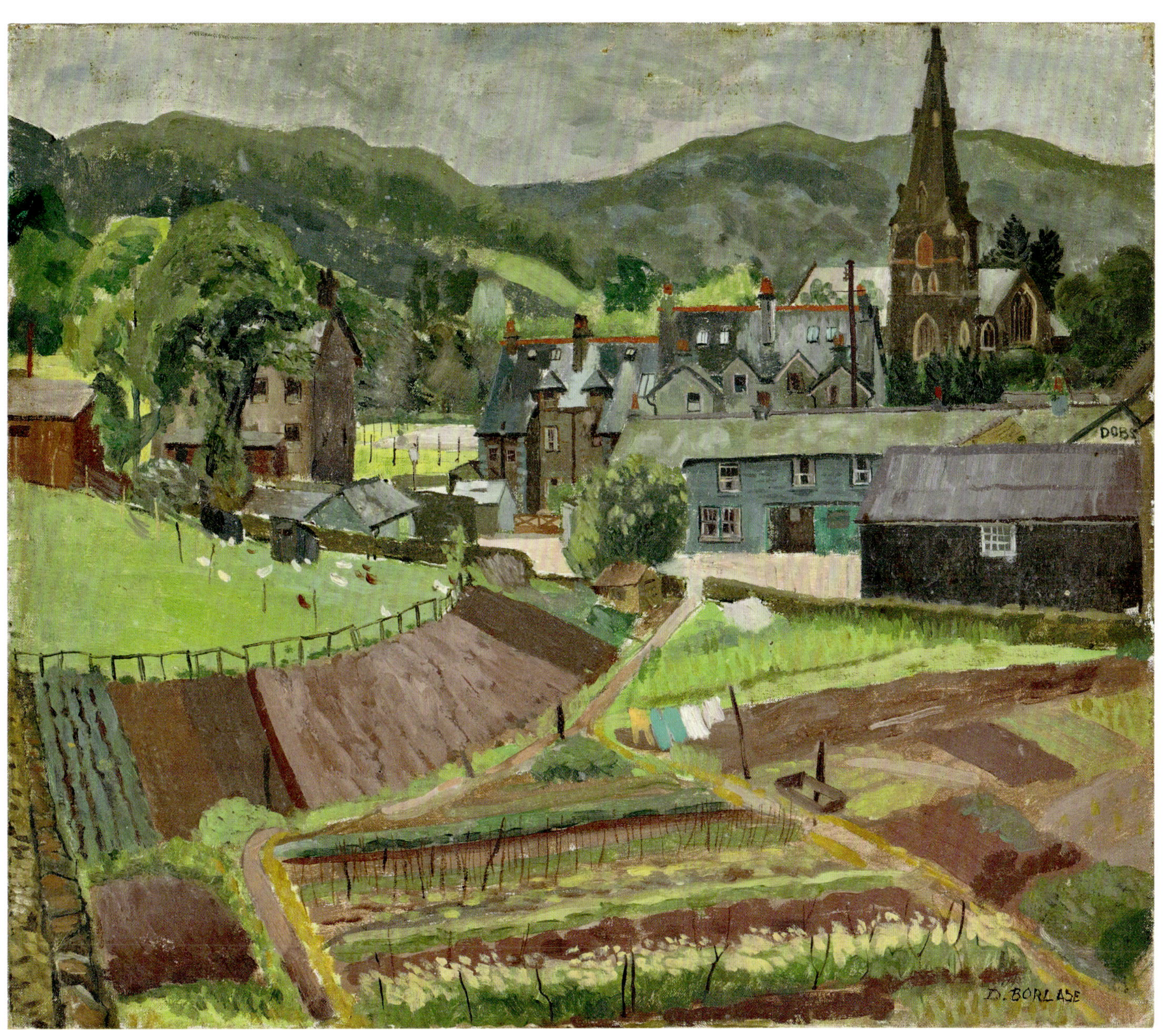

Cheyne Walk 1946

This painting was made on my Mother's return to London after the war. My parents lived in Chelsea. My father taught painting in the Art school. Not many of my Mother's paintings from this Era still exist, my father painted over them.

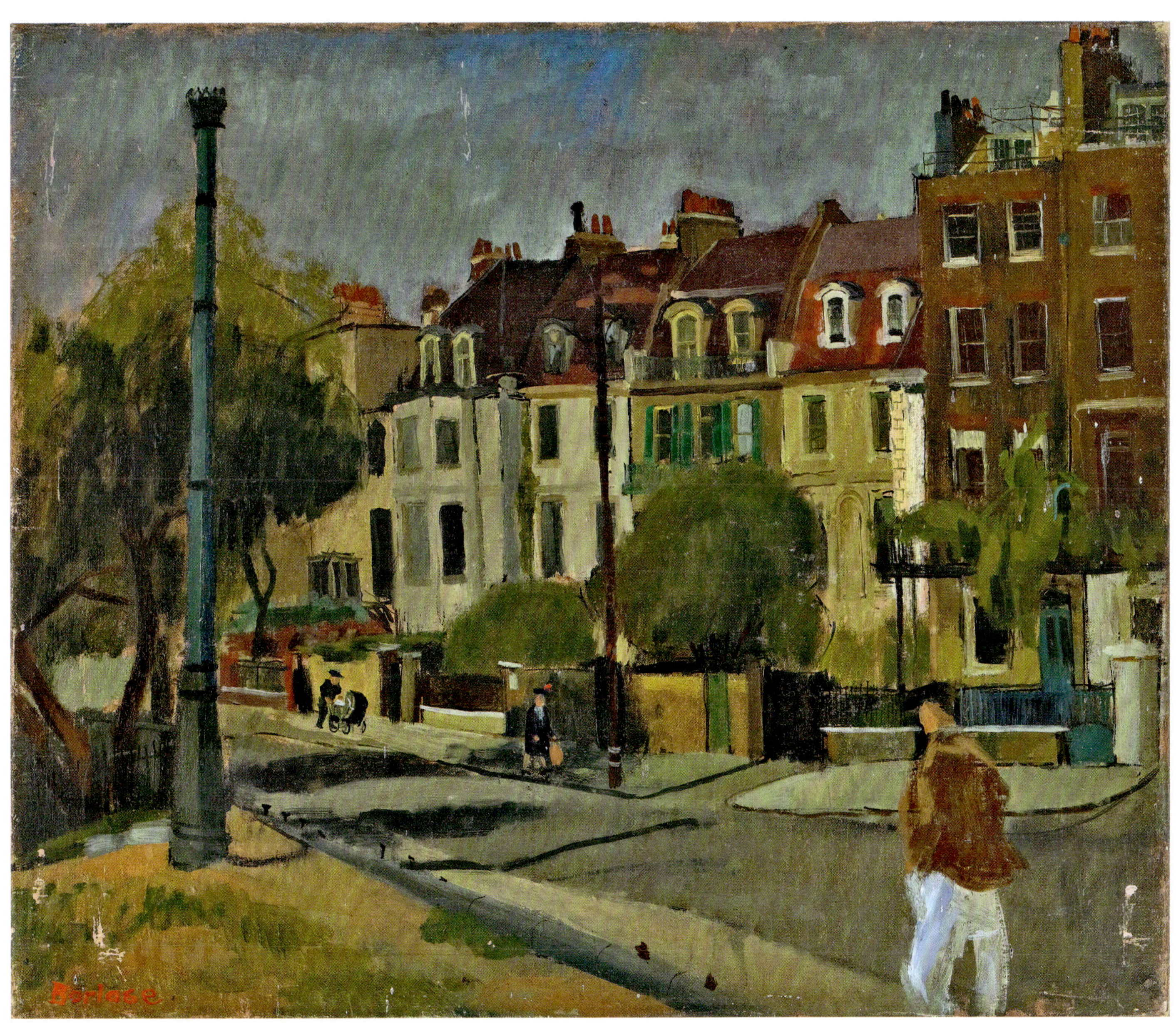

Still life circa 1948

This image represents early married life in post war Britain. It is a collection of unremarkable tins and bottles but it is beautifully painted and elegantly conceived.

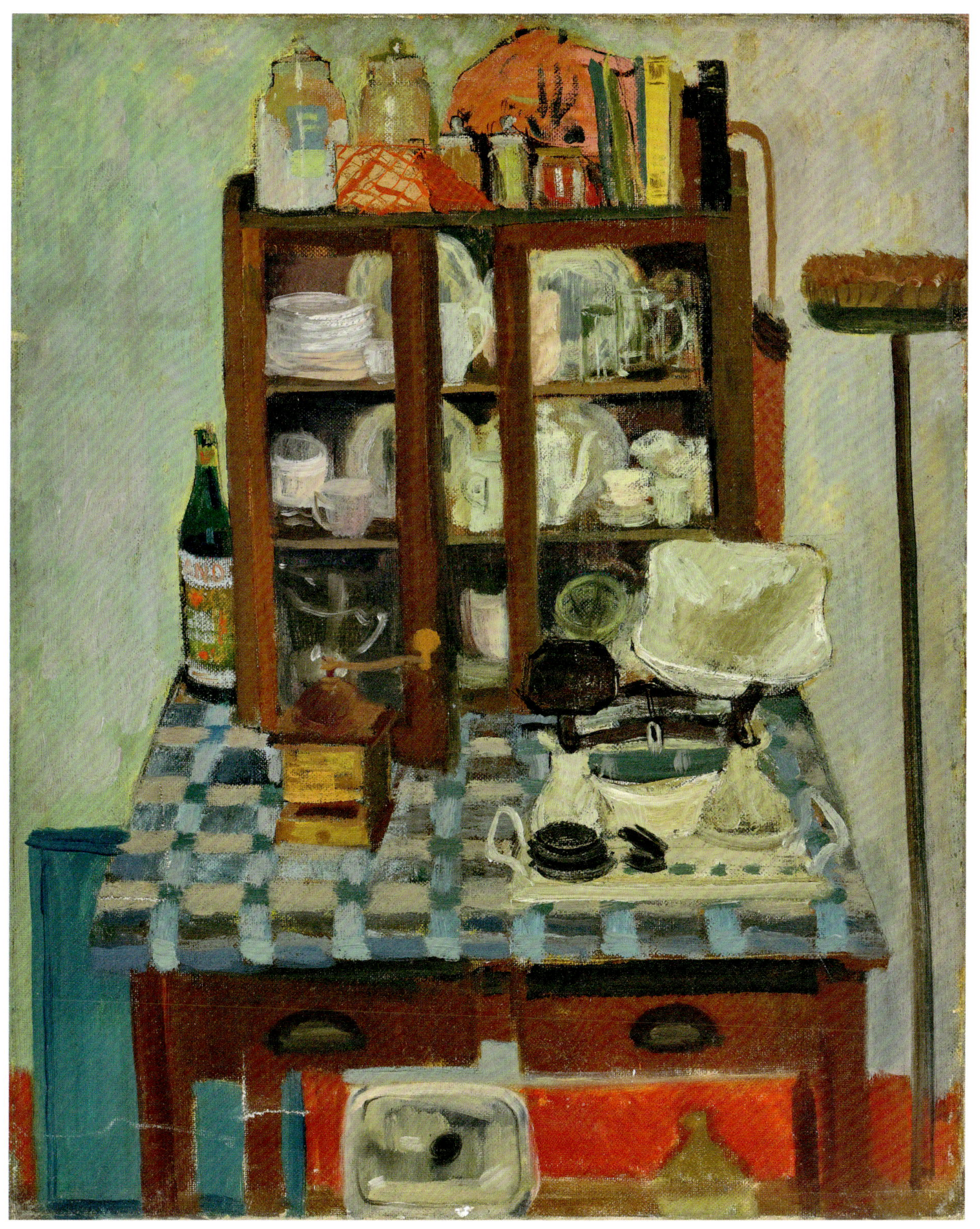

THE CONCRETE WORKS

1973

Deirdre had no studio. She would drive to locations the interested her, usually dismal back streets near the Thames on Grey day: The paintings were poetic but down beat. They represent a state of mind. She was an exile in suburbia inhabiting the edgelands of the ART WORLD

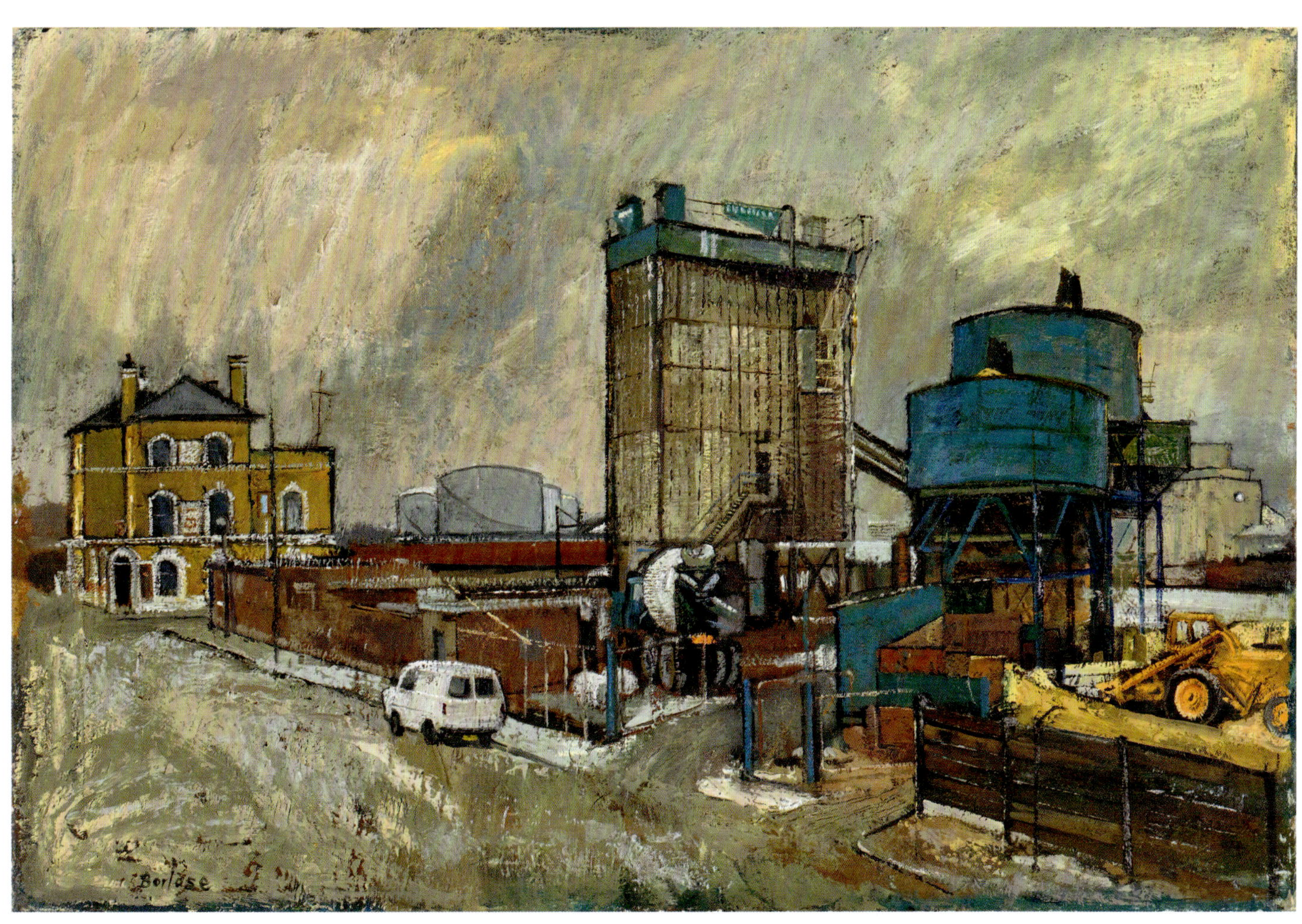

GASOMETERS BATTERSEA

1974

On Sunday mornings I would accompany
Deirdre on her painting trips. She would
turf me out of the car and set up her oil
paints on the passenger seat 'Go and play'
As I walked the streets she would paint
flicking the interior of the car with colour
The car was her, mobile,
Room of her own...

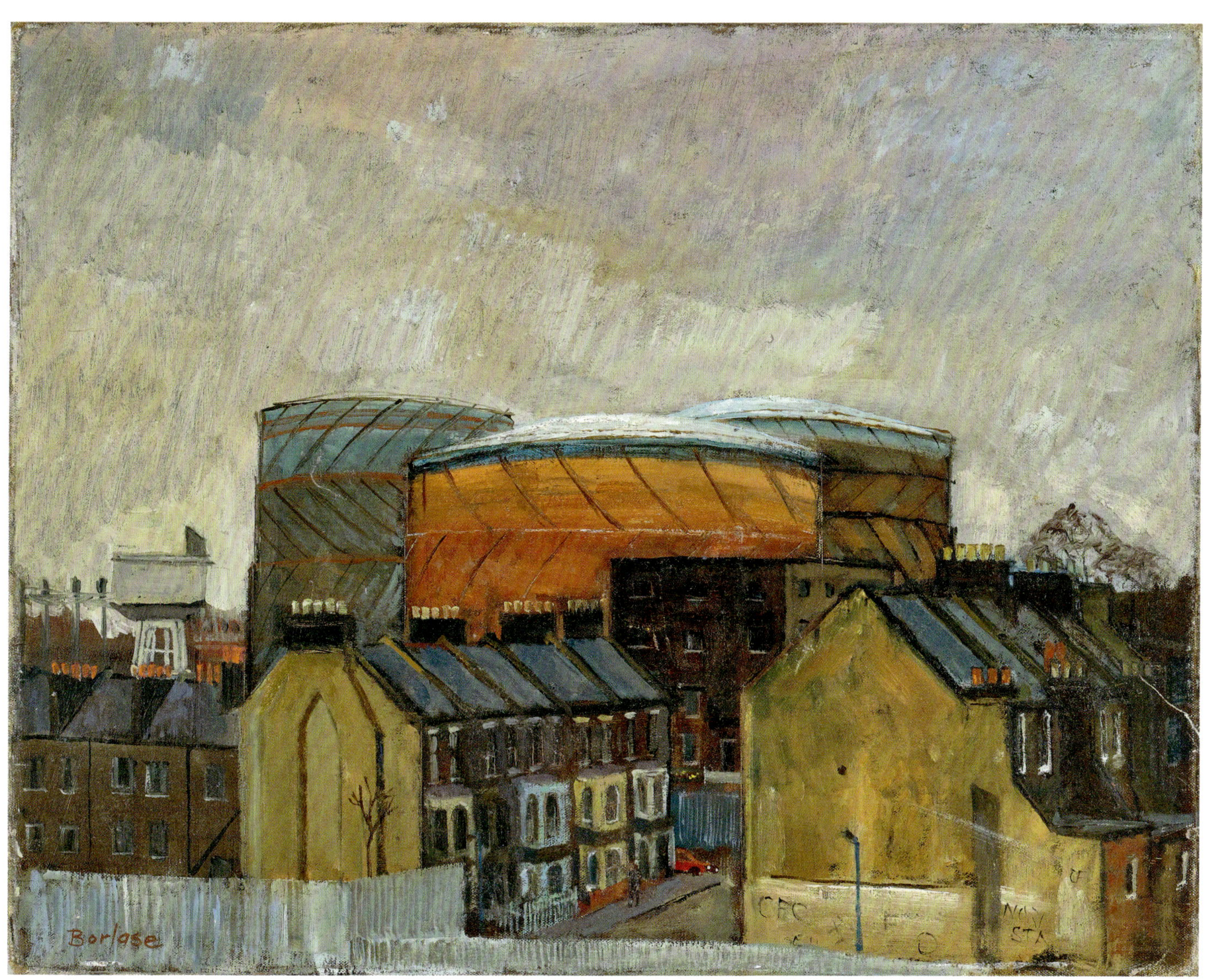

Borlase

Parsons Green 1977

My mother was born in 1925, a year before the Queen. Her life reflected the changes in Britain durring that time.

An increasing awareness and anger at the position of women. After the 50s & 60s when Deirdre had been distracted bringing up kids she set up a studio in our house in the late 70s and began to really Flourish and live as an Artist!

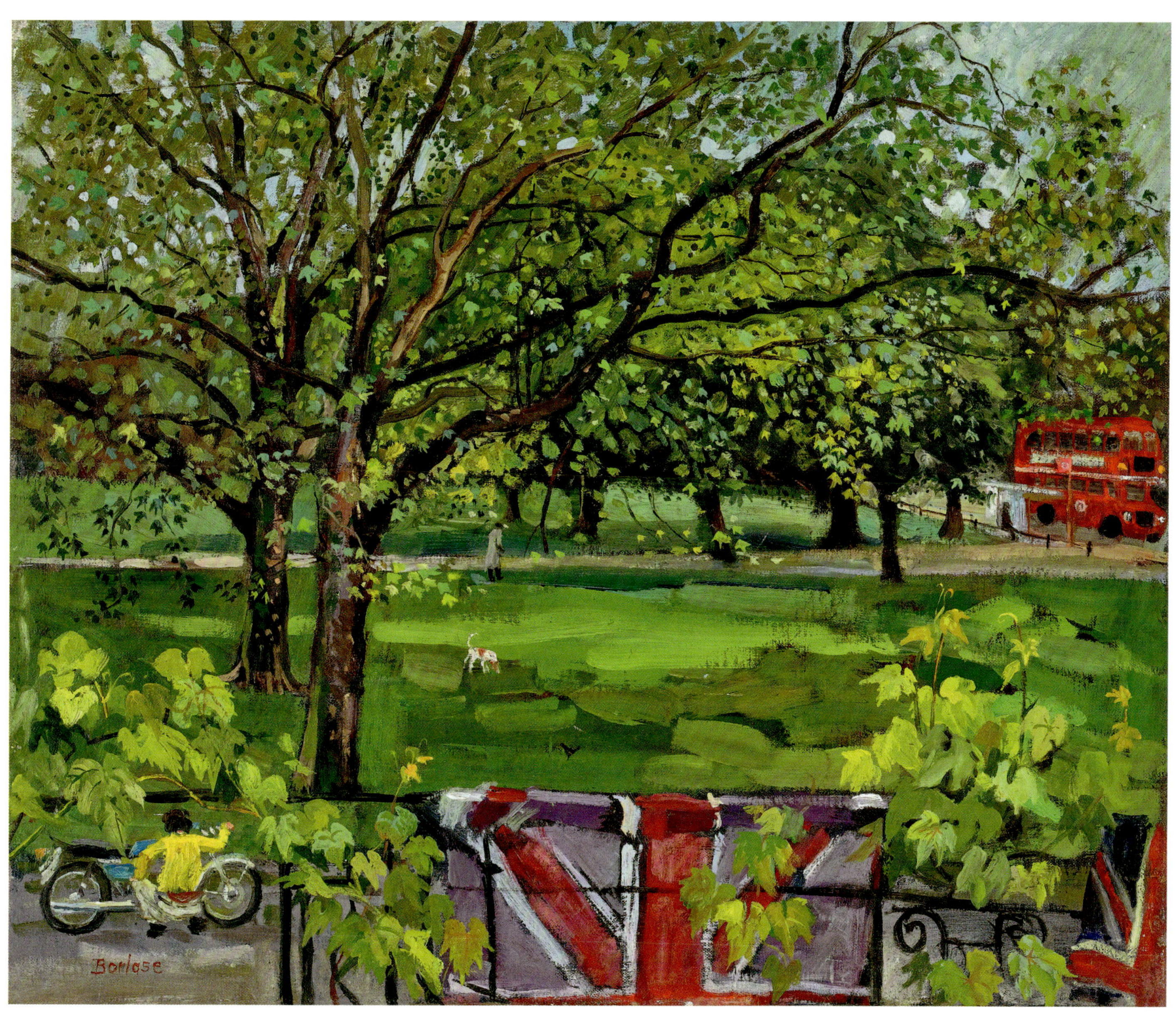
Borlase

Deirdre made this image of me in 1982. I remember posing for her but not quite like this. As she grew older she liked to experiment, there were always new things to do.

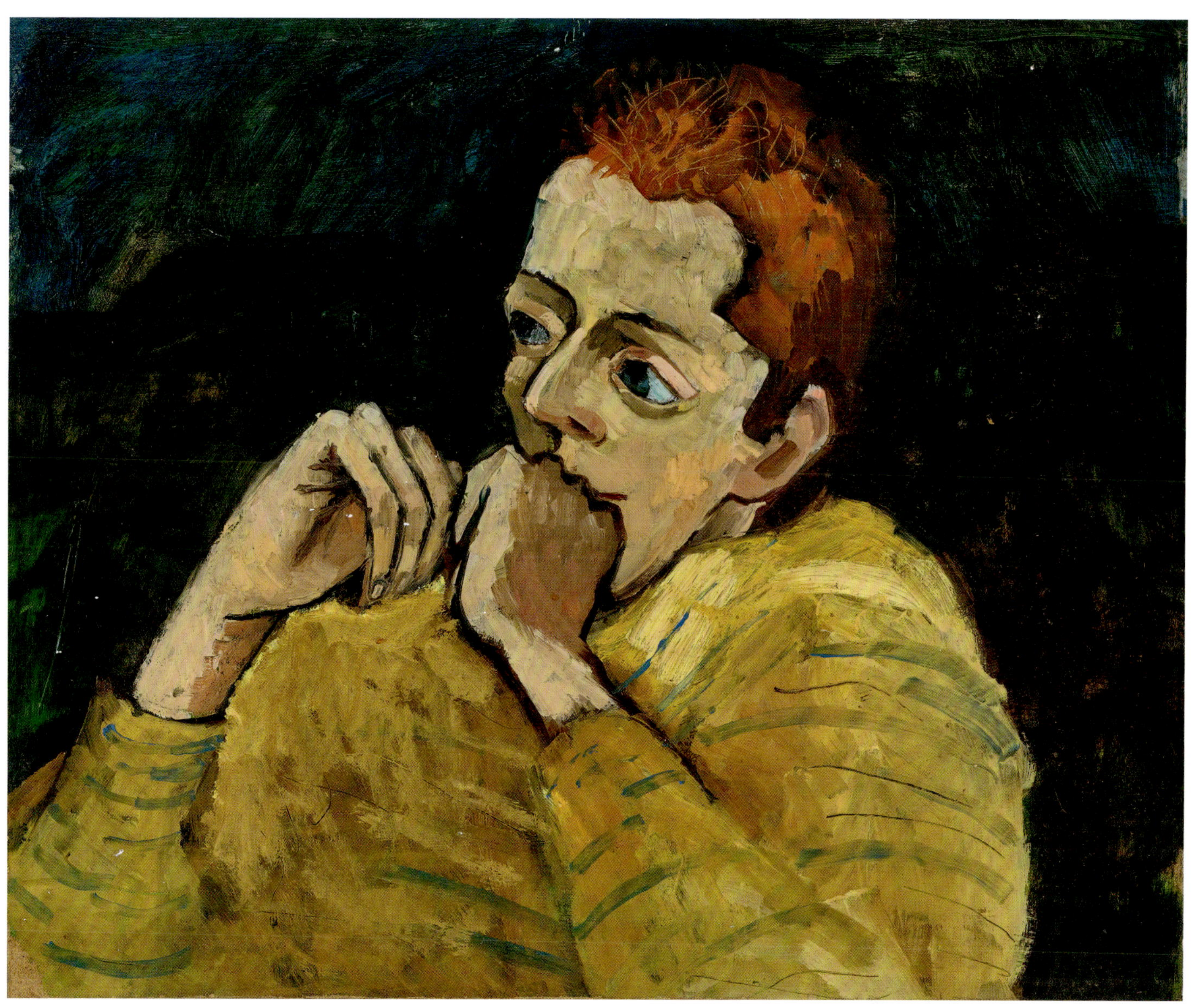

This is my soulpture of Deirdre. She taught me to draw. Start with the Christmas Pudding and end with your whole family celebrating on Christmas day

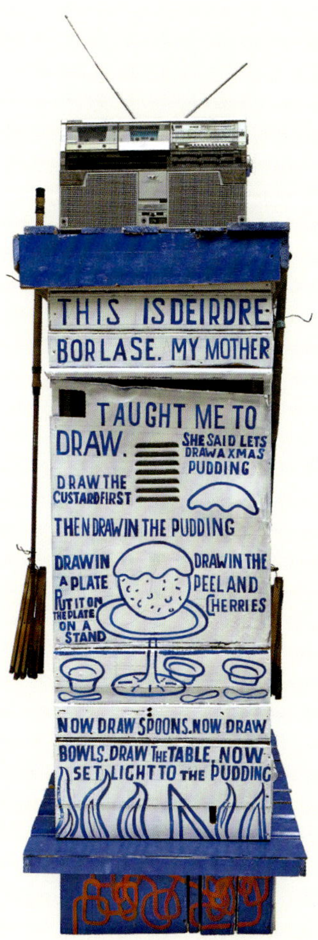

THIS IS DEIRDRE
BORLASE. MY MOTHER
TAUGHT ME TO
DRAW.
SHE SAID LETS
DRAW A XMAS
PUDDING
DRAW THE
CUSTARD FIRST
THEN DRAW IN THE PUDDING
DRAW IN A PLATE
DRAW IN THE PEEL AND CHERRIES
PUT IT ON THE PLATE ON A STAND
NOW DRAW SPOONS. NOW DRAW
BOWLS. DRAW THE TABLE. NOW
SET LIGHT TO THE PUDDING

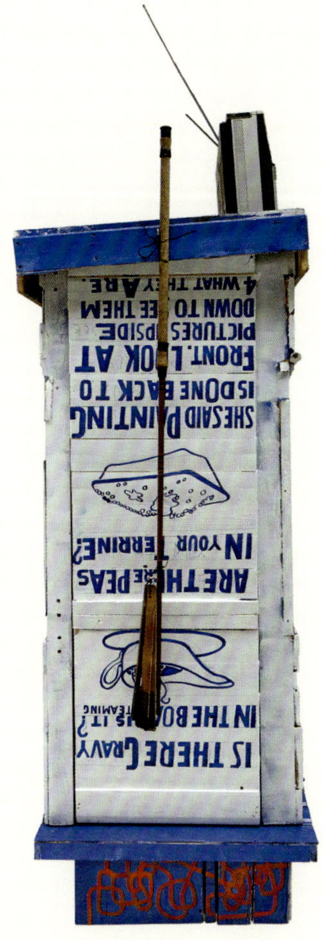

SHE'D PAINTING IS DONE BACK TO FRONT. LOOK AT PICTURES UPSIDE DOWN TO SEE THEM 4 WHAT THEY ARE.
ARE THE PEAS IN YOUR TERRINE?
IS THERE GRAVY IN THE BOAT? IS IT STEAMING

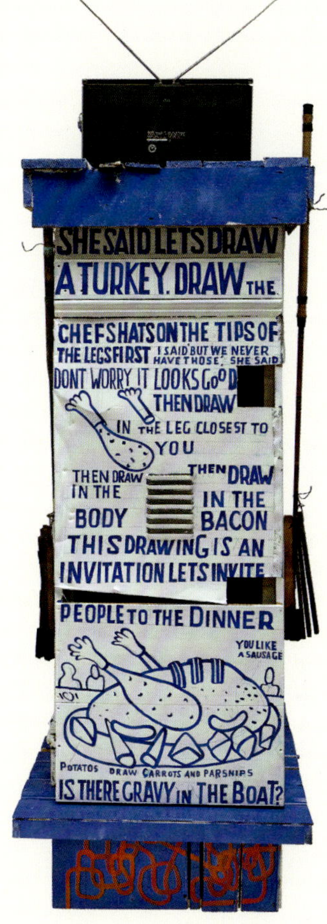

SHE SAID LETS DRAW
A TURKEY. DRAW THE
CHEFS HATS ON THE TIPS OF
THE LEGS FIRST I SAID BUT WE NEVER
HAVE THOSE, SHE SAID
DONT WORRY IT LOOKS GOOD
THEN DRAW
IN THE LEG CLOSEST TO
YOU
THEN DRAW
IN THE
BODY
THEN DRAW
IN THE
BACON
THIS DRAWING IS AN
INVITATION LETS INVITE
PEOPLE TO THE DINNER
YOU LIKE A SAUSAGE
POTATOS DRAW CARROTS AND PARSNIPS
IS THERE GRAVY IN THE BOAT?

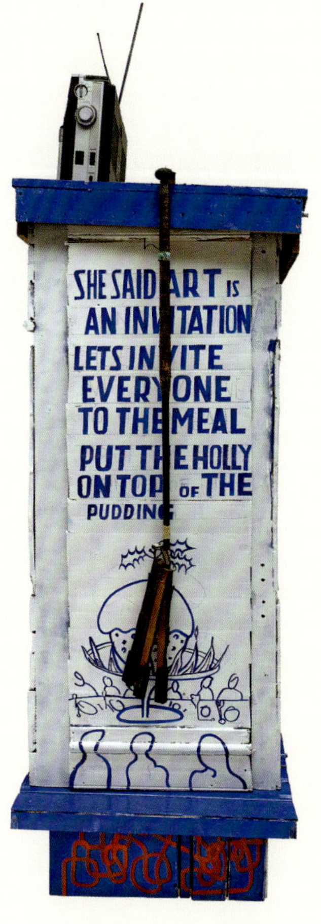

SHE SAID ART IS
AN INVITATION
LETS INVITE
EVERYONE
TO THE MEAL
PUT THE HOLLY
ON TOP OF THE
PUDDING

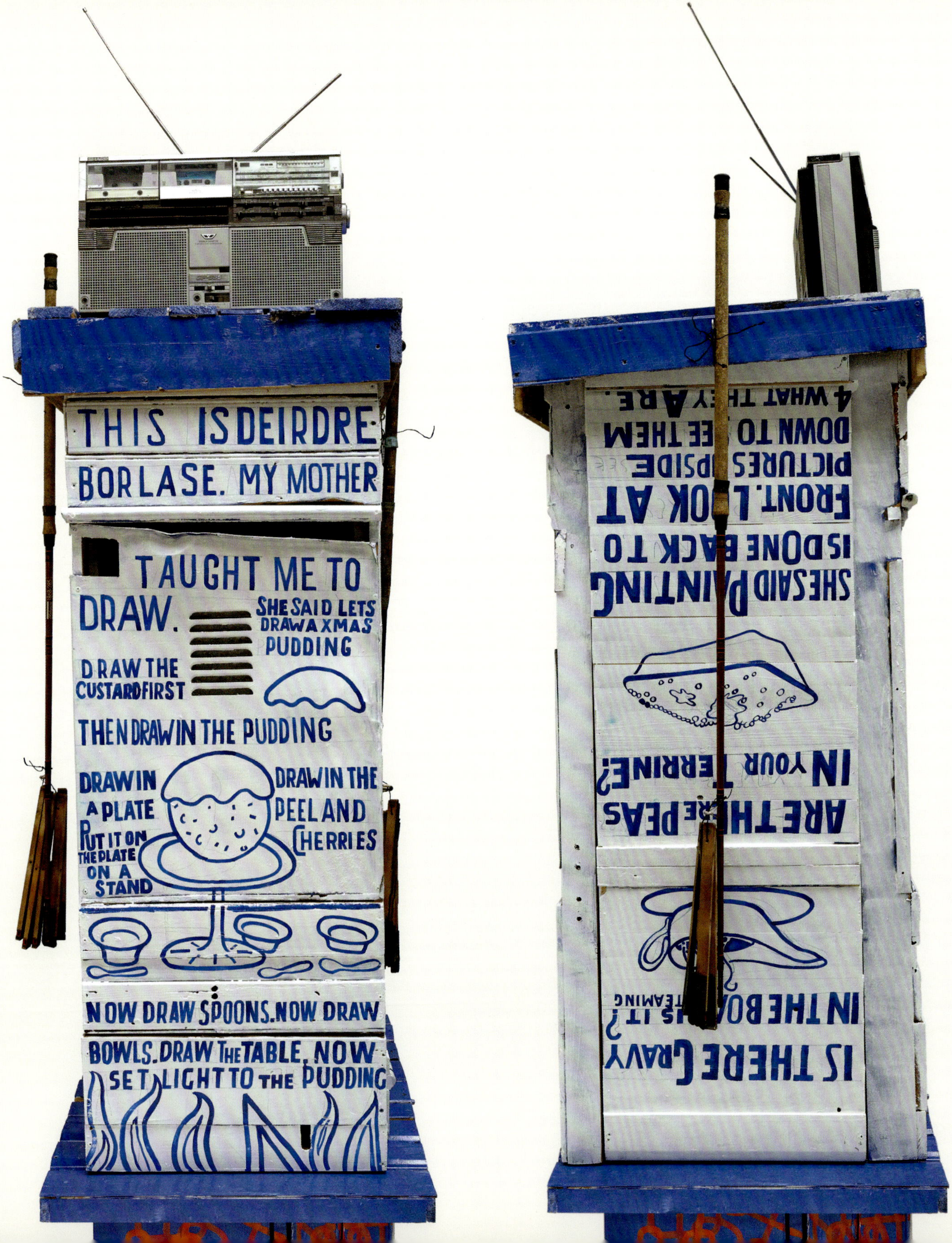

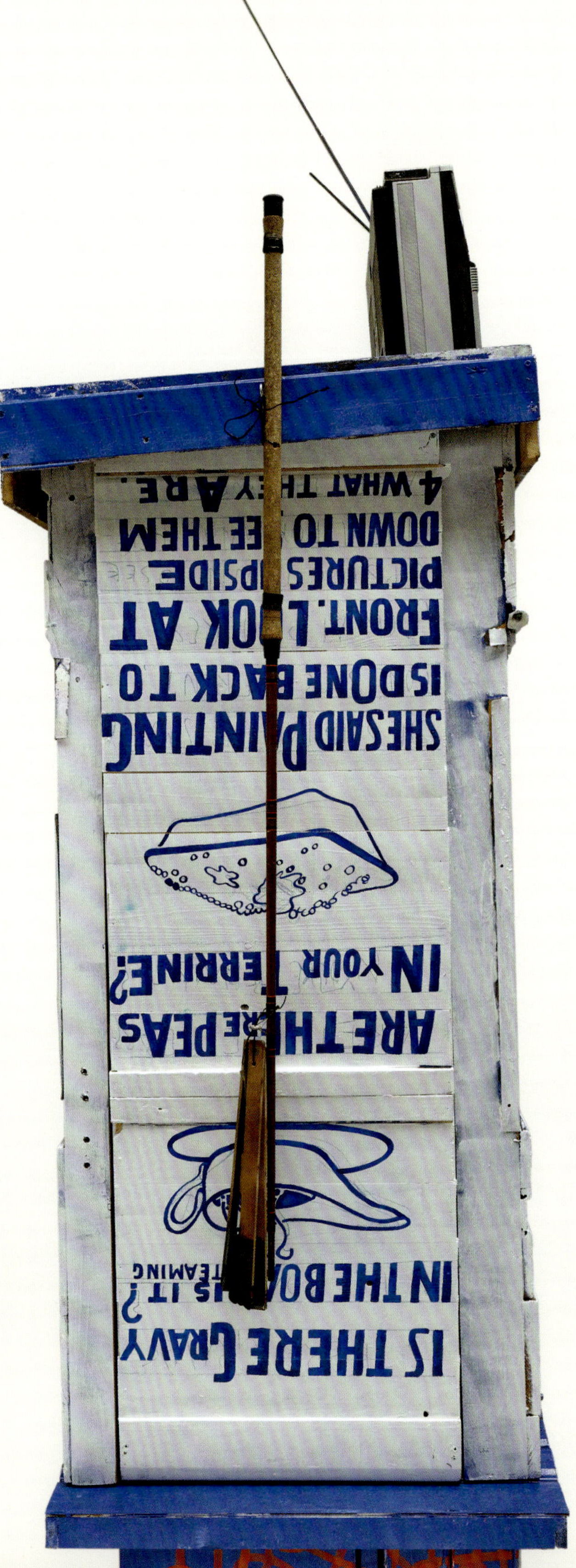

THIS IS DEIRDRE
BORLASE. MY MOTHER
TAUGHT ME TO
DRAW. SHE SAID LETS
DRAW A XMAS PUDDING
DRAW THE CUSTARD FIRST
THEN DRAW IN THE PUDDING
DRAW IN A PLATE
PUT IT ON THE PLATE ON A STAND
DRAW IN THE PEEL AND CHERRIES
NOW DRAW SPOONS. NOW DRAW
BOWLS. DRAW THE TABLE. NOW SET LIGHT TO THE PUDDING
SHE SAID PAINTING IS DONE BACK TO FRONT. LOOK AT PICTURES UPSIDE DOWN TO SEE THEM 4 WHAT THEY ARE.
ARE THERE PEAS IN YOUR TERRINE?
IS THERE GRAVY IN THE BOWLS IS IT STEAMING?

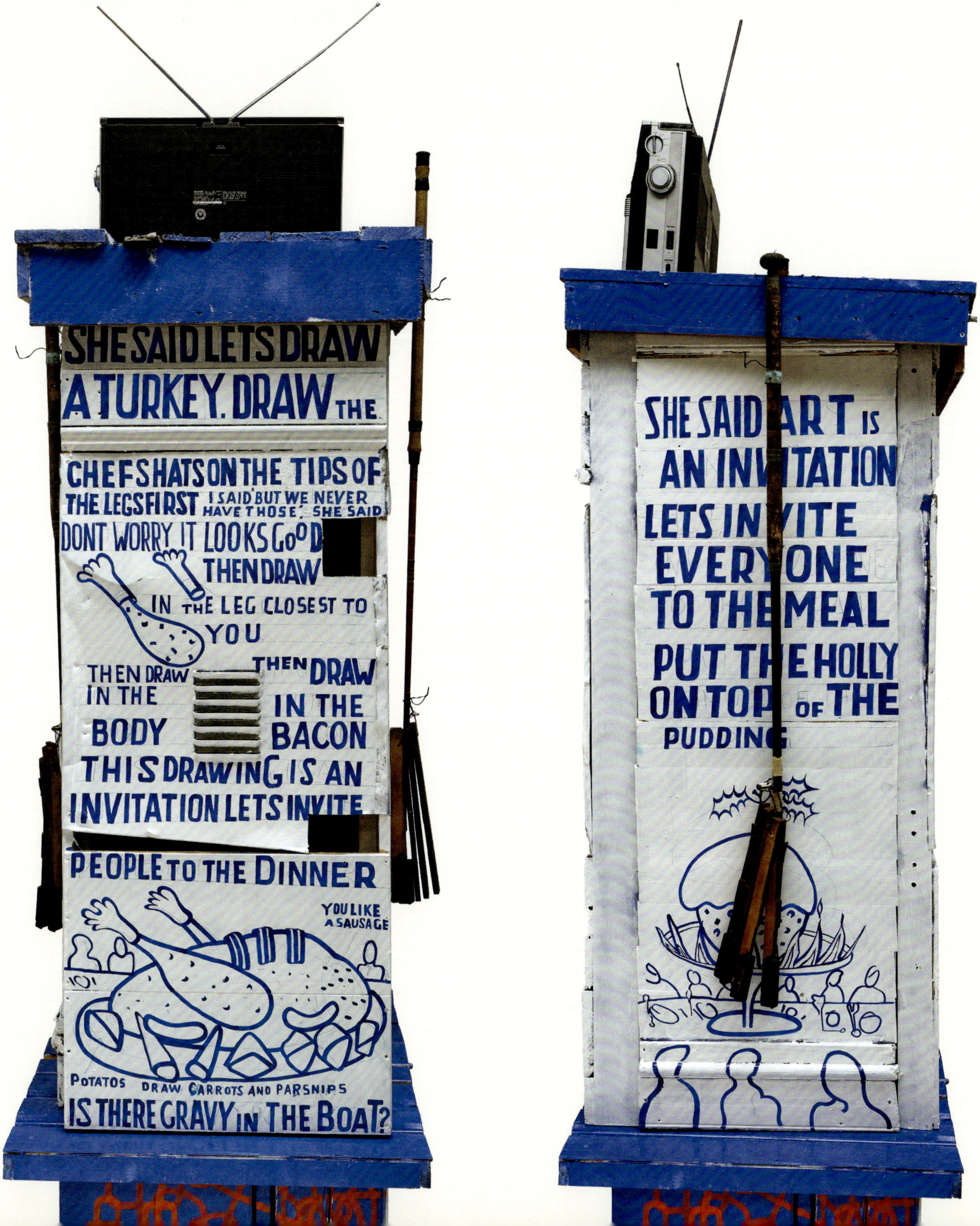

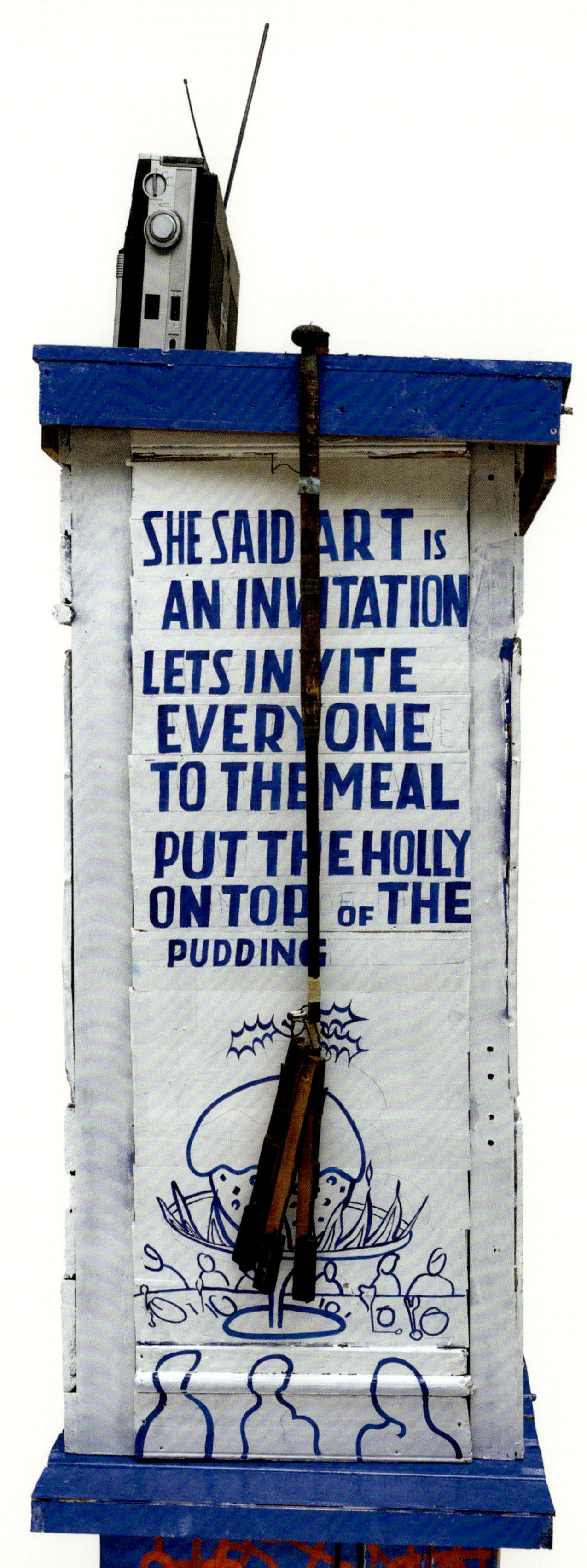

SHE SAID LETS DRAW
A TURKEY. DRAW THE
CHEFS HATS ON THE TIPS OF
THE LEGS FIRST I SAID BUT WE NEVER
HAVE THOSE SHE SAID
DONT WORRY IT LOOKS GOOD
THEN DRAW
IN THE LEG CLOSEST TO
YOU
THEN DRAW THEN DRAW
IN THE IN THE
BODY BACON
THIS DRAWING IS AN
INVITATION LETS INVITE
PEOPLE TO THE DINNER
YOU LIKE
A SAUSAGE
POTATOS DRAW CARROTS AND PARSNIPS
IS THERE GRAVY IN THE BOAT?
SHE SAID ART IS
AN INVITATION
LETS INVITE
EVERYONE
TO THE MEAL
PUT THE HOLLY
ON TOP OF THE
PUDDING

Joshua Reynolds was the 1st president of the RA and an early art educator. The RA schools was the first Art school of its kind and still educates artists Today

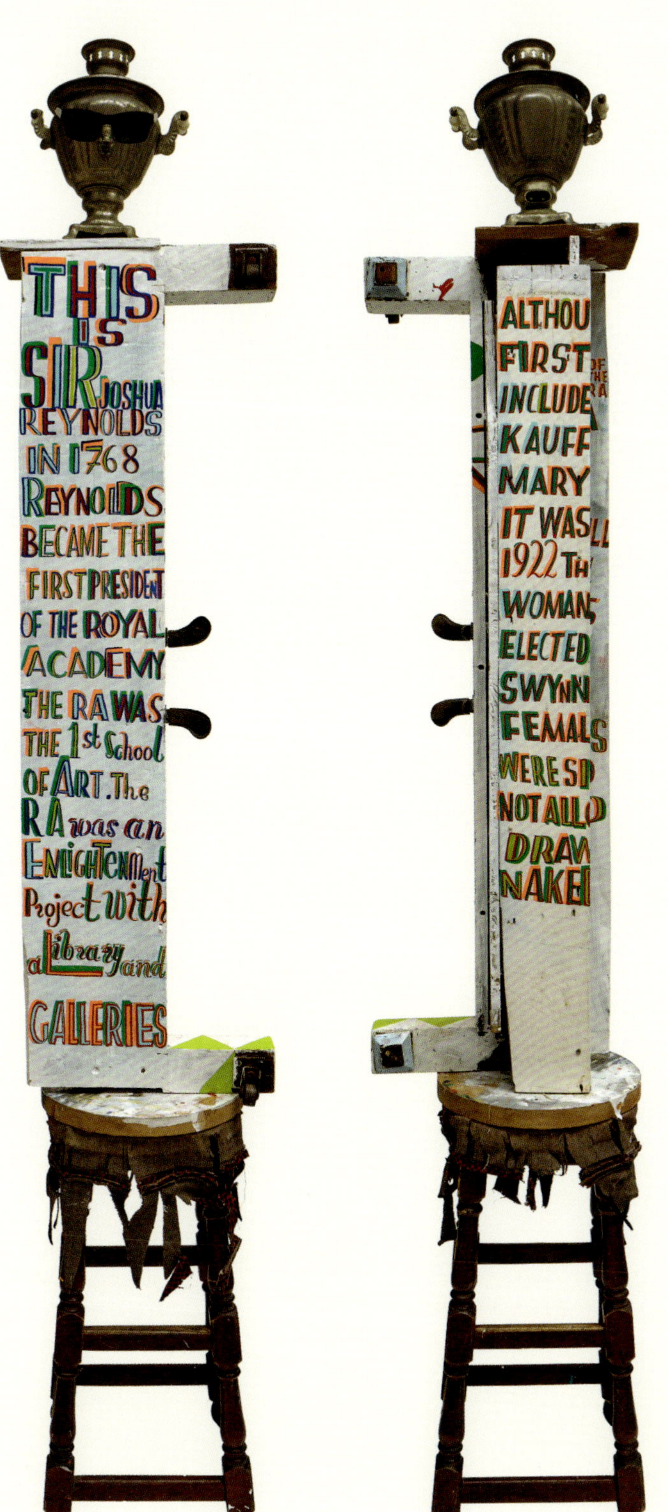

THIS IS SIR JOSHUA REYNOLDS IN 1768 REYNOLDS BECAME THE FIRST PRESIDENT OF THE ROYAL ACADEMY THE RA WAS THE 1st School OF ART. The RA was an Enlightenment Project with a Library and GALLERIES
ALTHOU FIRST OF THE RA INCLUDE KAUFF MARY IT WASL 1922 TH WOMAN ELECTED SWYNN FEMALS WERE SD NOT ALLO DRAW NAKE

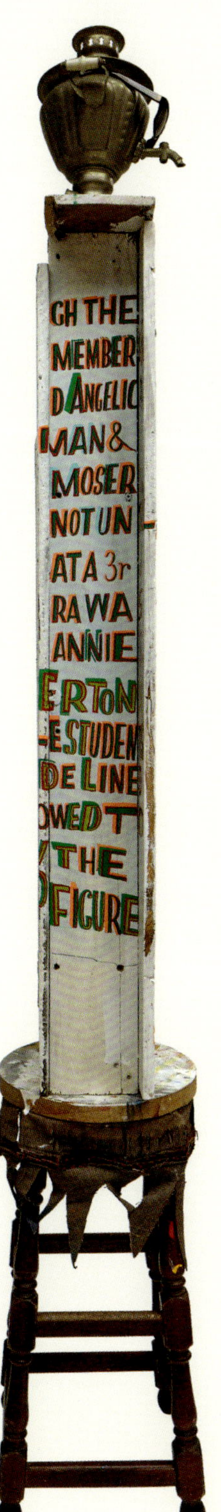

GH THE MEMBER D ANGELIC MAN & MOSER NOT UN AT A 3r RA WA ANNIE ERTON E STUDEM DE LINE OWED T THE FIGURE

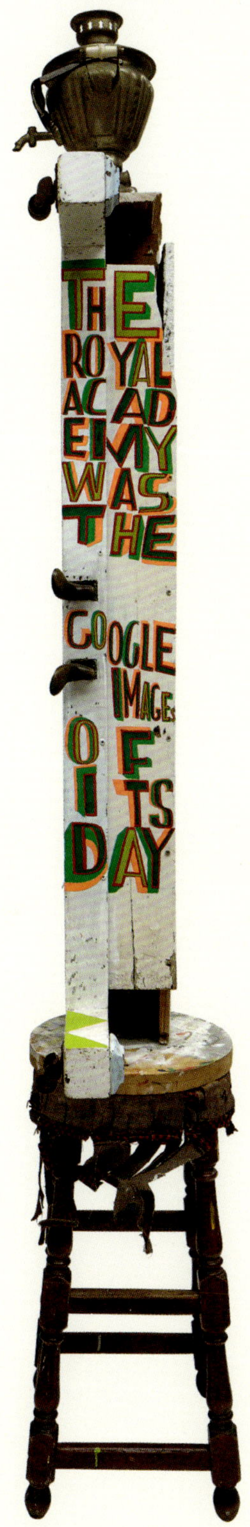

THE ROYAL ACADEMY WAS THE GOOGLE IMAGES OF ITS DAY

Angelica Kaufman was a founder member of the RA. My wife Jessica Voorsanger has painted her for this sculpture along with portrait of inspiring women Artists of the past and of today

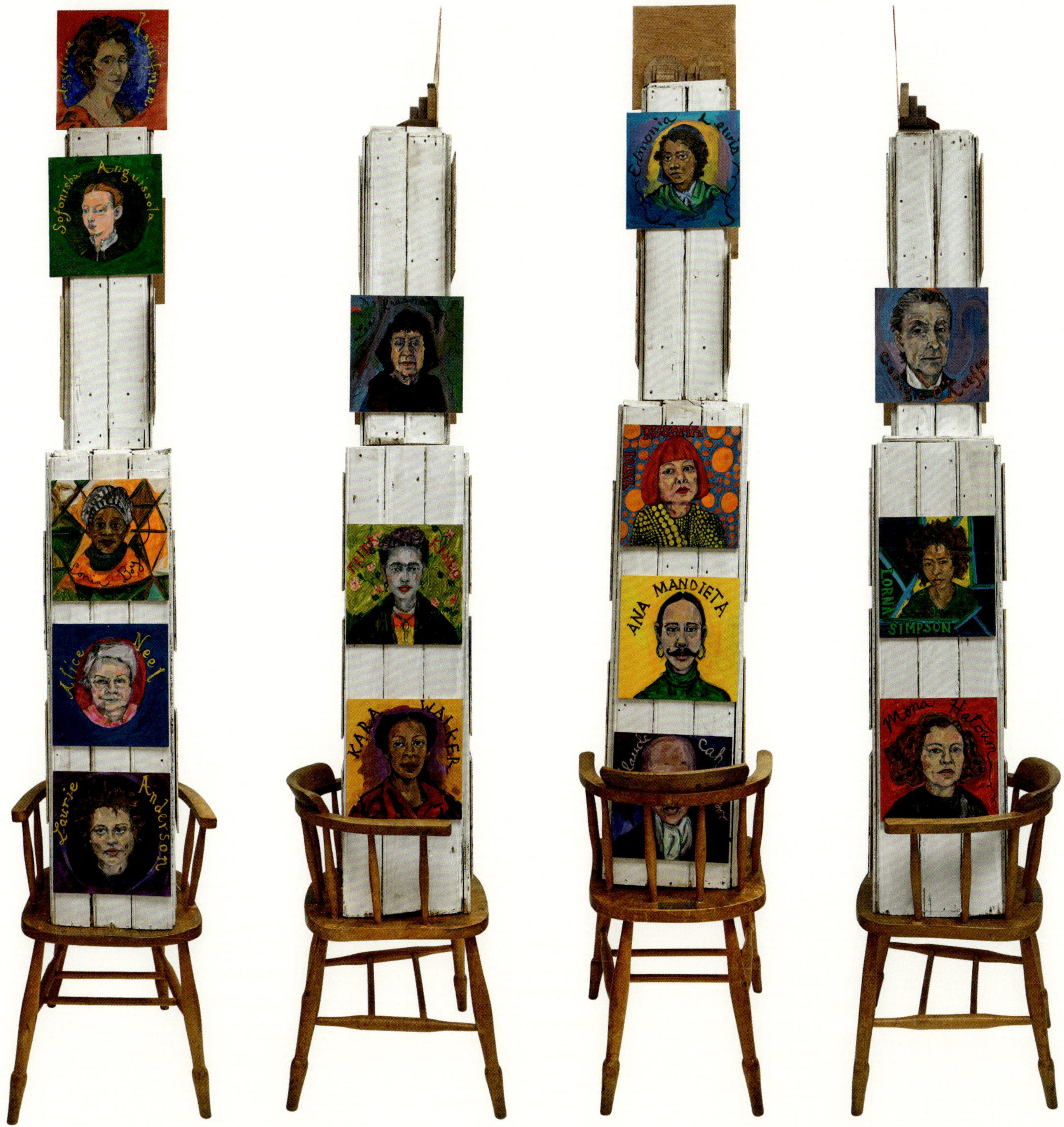

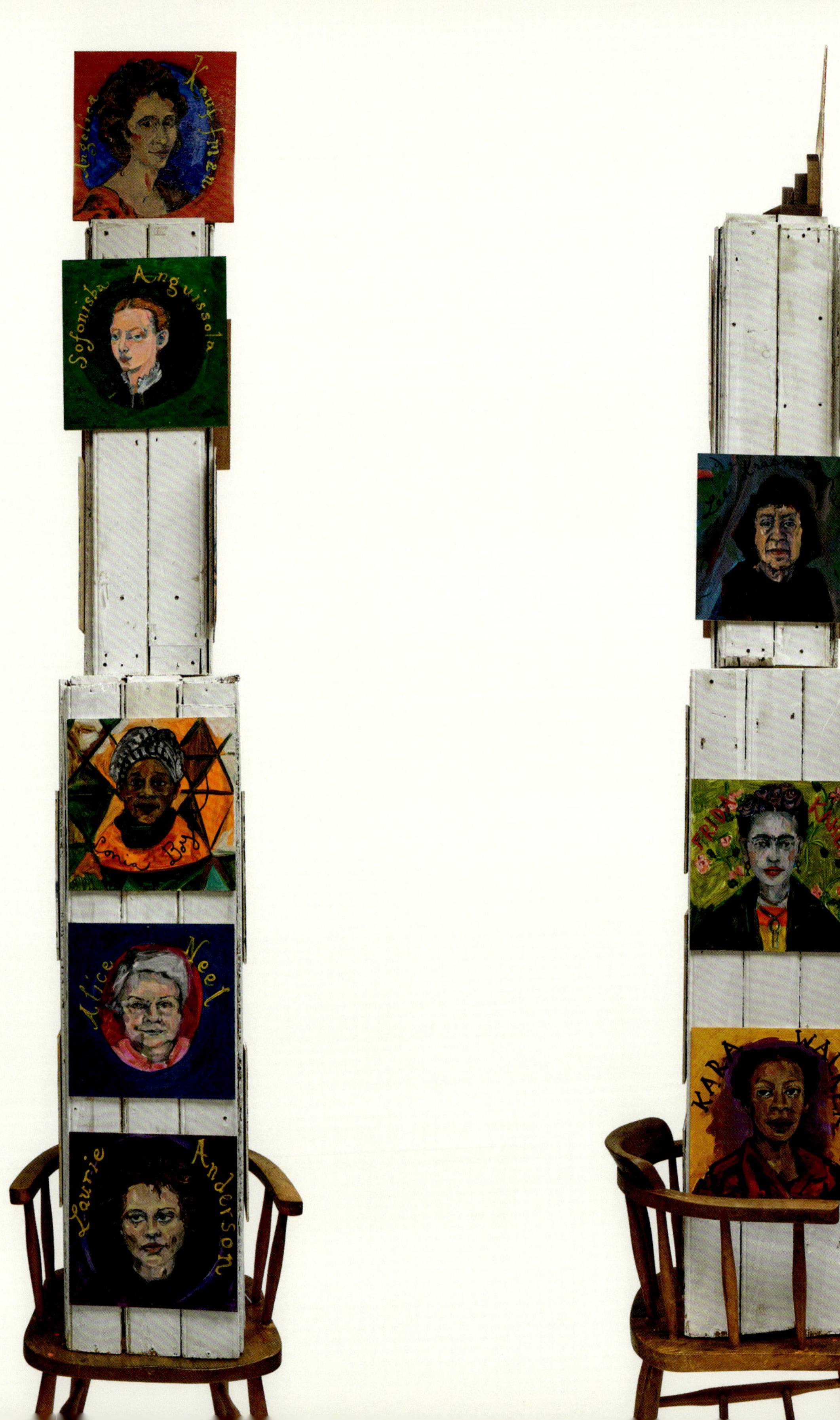

Angelica Kauffman
Sofonisba Anguissola
Lois Mailou Jones
Alice Neel
Laurie Anderson
Frida Kahlo
KARA WALKER

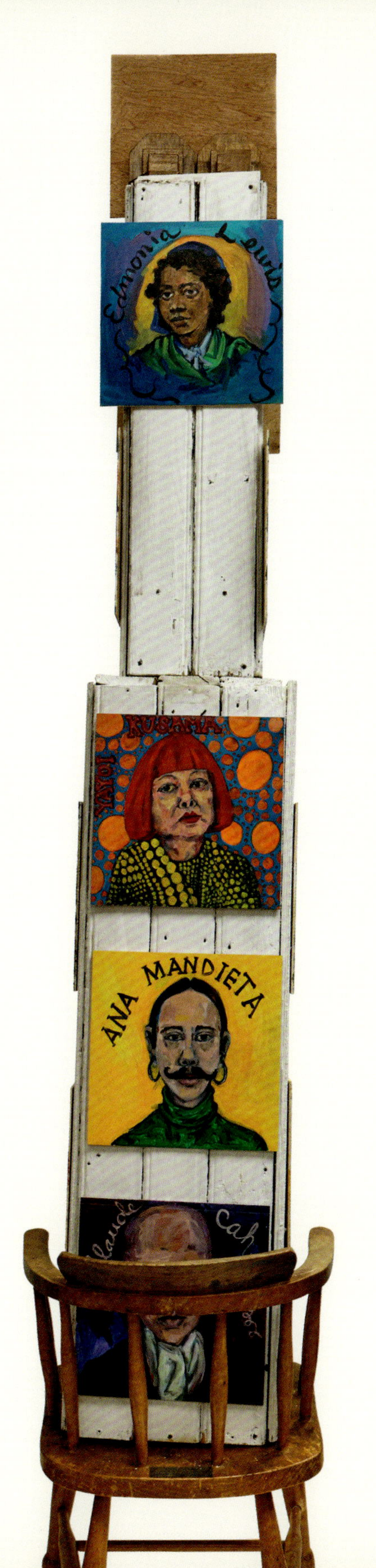

Edmonia Lewis
YAYOI KUSAMA
ANA MANDIETA
Claude Cahun

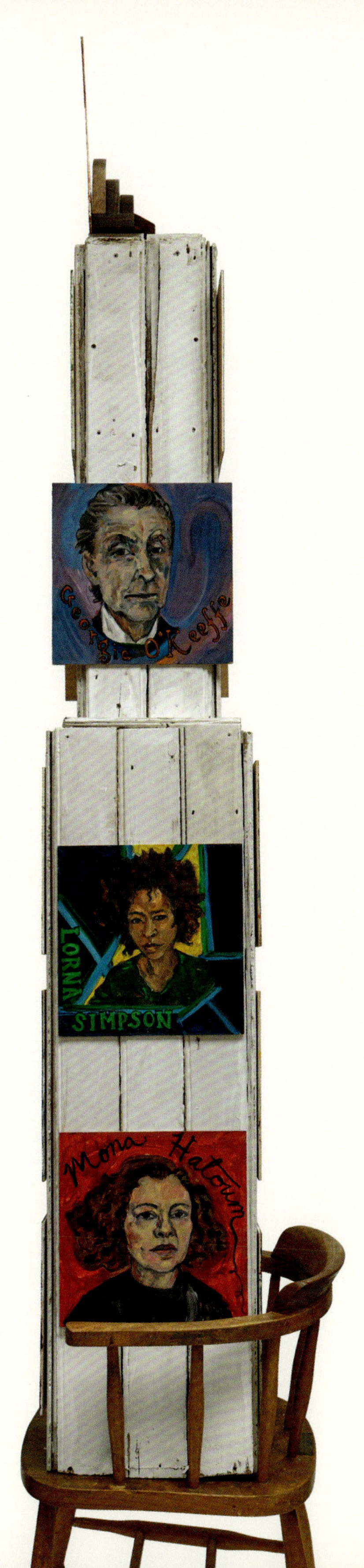

Georgia O'Keeffe
LORNA SIMPSON
Mona Hatoum

Mary Moser was the only other female founder. My daughter Ella Voorsanger-Bri... wrote her dissertation on Feminist Ephemera. She ha... made a Mary Moser fanzine and has paisted it to this sculptur...

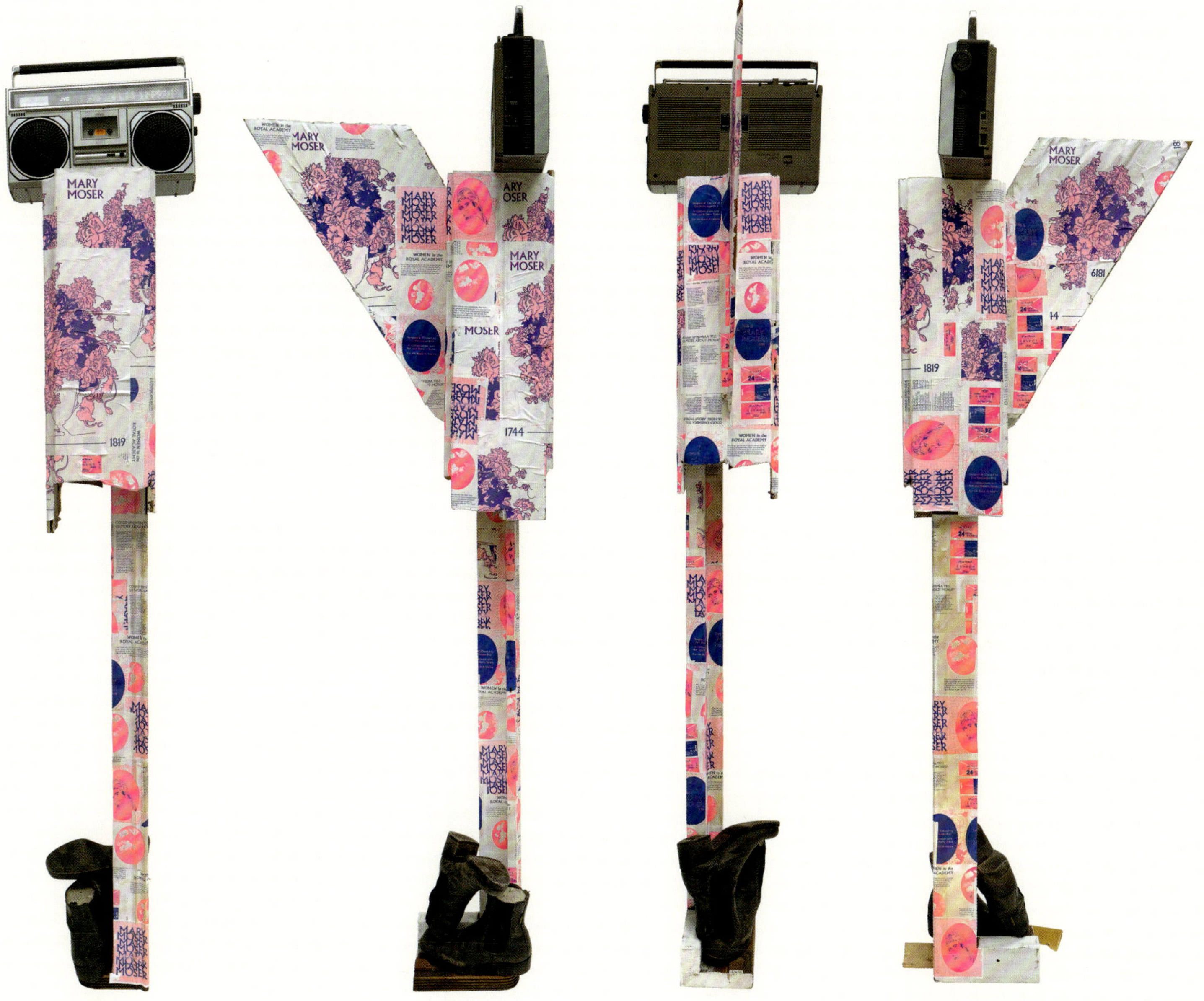

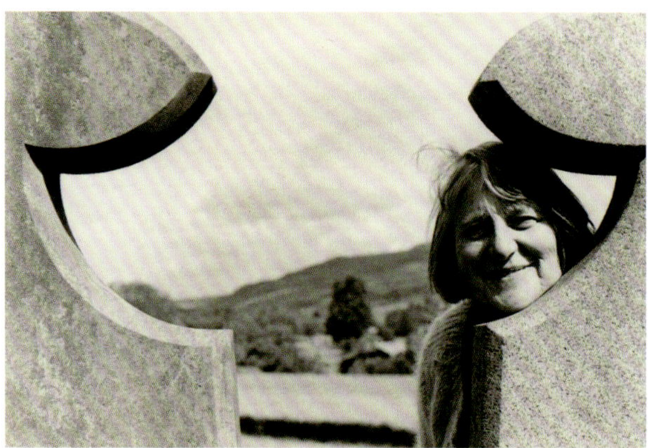

Deirdre Borlase
25 July 1925 – 21 July 2018

Limited edition
This book is published in a limited edition of 250 copies, signed and numbered by the artist. The edition includes a limited edition print (Bob and Roberta Smith, *The Secret to a Good Life*, 2018. Offset lithograph on 300gsm Munken Polar Rough, 22.5 x 22.5 cm) and a limited edition zine (Etta Voorsanger-Brill, *This is Mary Moser*, 2018. Risograph, 14.8 x 10.5 cm).

Royal Academy Publications
Florence Dassonville, Production Coordinator
Rosie Hore, Project Editor
Carola Krueger, Production Manager
Peter Sawbridge, Editorial Director
Nick Tite, Publisher

Design: Patrick Morrissey, Unlimited
Photography: DawkinsColour (John Bodkin), London
Colour Origination: DawkinsColour
Printed by Gomer Press in Wales

British Library Cataloguing-in-Publication Data
A catalogue record for this book is available from the British Library

ISBN 978-1-910350-83-6

Distributed outside the United States and Canada by ACC Art Books Ltd, Sandy Lane, Old Martlesham, Woodbridge, Suffolk IP12 4SD

Distributed in the United States and Canada by ARTBOOK | D.A.P., 155 Sixth Avenue, New York NY 10013